QUILTS 2000

AUSTRALIA CELEBRATES

QUILTS 2000

AUSTRALIA CELEBRATES

KAREN FAIL AND DIANNE FINNEGAN

Published in Australia in 2000
by QUILTS 2000 Inc.
P.O. Box 257 Frenchs Forest 1640
www.Quilts2000.org.au
info@Quilts2000.org.au

Quilts 2000 - Australia Celebrates

ISBN 0 646 39523 8

Printed by Kingswood Press
PO Box 3121 Logan City 4114
Queensland, Australia 1620

Trade Distribution
Sally Milner Publishing Pty Ltd
PO Box 2104, Bowral,
NSW, Australia 2576
Phone: 61 2 48624212
Fax: 61 2 48624214

Distribution US/UK/Japan
Quilters' Resource Inc.
P.O. Box 148850
Chicago IL60614 U.S.A.
Phone: ++ 1 773 278 5695
Fax: ++ 1 773 278 1348

PARALYMPIC GAMES SYDNEY 2000 TM ©

Official Fundraising Project

Dedicated to the Paralympians whose power performance and pursuit of perfection have inspired this project.

Contents

With just the

thread of an idea,

QUILTS 2000

proposed a

project that was

simple yet

ambitious

With just the thread of an idea of using quilts to contribute in some way to the Sydney 2000 Paralympic Games, our small group of ten, which was QUILTS 2000 Inc, proposed a project in 1998 that was simple yet ambitious.

What developed in the next three years surprised us all.

While links between quilts and elite sport are not new (among them Atlanta in 1996), in Sydney, Australia we chose to raise funds for the Paralympic Games from the sale of donated quilts. This was the first time such an approach had been taken; in the process QUILTS 2000 developed into the world's biggest fund-raising event using quilts.

The Internet allowed for a virtual quilt exhibition, twenty-four hours a day for the life of the project, and provided an ever-increasing worldwide market. With images of all 630 quilts in the collection, *www.Quilts2000.org.au* rapidly became one of the world's largest quilting sites, being listed in the top one hundred craft websites in Australia.

QUILTS 2000 is part of the Paralympic Arts Festival at Sydney Olympic Park. The spectacle of the collection on show during the Sydney 2000 Paralympic Games October 18—29, is an exciting prospect.

From quilt and book sales QUILTS 2000 Inc anticipated raising AUD$500,000 for the Sydney 2000 Paralympic Games.

It has been an honour and a privilege to be associated with such an inspirational project.

Margaret Wright
Chairman
QUILTS 2000 Inc.
Sydney Australia,
June, 2000

CONTENTS

The aim was twofold—

to raise funds for the

Sydney 2000 Paralympic

Games and to raise

awareness of the Games

throughout Australia

Installation of QUILTS 2000 in the Presiding
Officers' Exhibition Area, Parliament House,
Canberra, April, 2000

QUILTS 2000 comprises a numbered collection of 630 quilts, made and donated by Australians to raise funds for the Sydney 2000 Paralympic Games and in doing so, to raise awareness of the event. The quilts have entered into the Australian memory as snapshots celebrating Sydney, the Australian way of life, and the performance ideals of the Paralympics. The collection is a pageant of patchwork, and every person who made a quilt, and each person who bought one helped create the spectacle and the history. The significance of the quilts themselves is part of their value—they are important 'documents' of a landmark occasion, the Paralympic Games of 2000.

In 1998, a group of Sydney quiltmakers who were interested in contributing to the Sydney 2000 Games, came together to coordinate their efforts. Their reasons for involvement varied, but all were motivated to add a cultural dimension to the sporting event. They saw it as a great opportunity to showcase Australia for the world, through the medium of quilts. After consideration, they decided to put their fundraising efforts behind the Paralympic Games which was not as heavily subsidised by the Government and was attracting less sponsorship. Their fundraising target was AUD$500,000.

The endorsement of the project by the Sydney 2000 Paralympic Organising Committee (SPOC) made QUILTS 2000 one of only two Official Community Projects. Lois Appleby, Chief Executive Officer of SPOC, signed the letter confirming acceptance of the project in 1998. QUILTS 2000 was up and running!

The aim was twofold: to raise funds for the Sydney 2000 Paralympic Games and to raise awareness of the Games throughout Australia. The goals were made possible with the backing of Brother International (Australasia); their generous financial sponsorship made an Australia-wide project feasible.

To publicise the project required media sponsorship, and two Australian quilting magazines, *Australian Patchwork and Quilting* and *Down Under Quilts,* enthusiastically supported the venture and unstintingly gave editorial support. To reach the wider community beyond quiltmakers, *The Australian Women's Weekly* agreed to become the general media sponsor. Expertise Events proved a valuable supporter by giving the project space at its State craft shows.

Not only were the quilts displayed in exhibitions across Australia, but from the time of the launch, all the quilts were shown on the QUILTS 2000 web site at www.Quilts2000.org.au

Launch of the QUILTS 2000 project at Customs House, Circular Quay, February 1999

The first priority was to publicise QUILTS 2000 to quiltmakers and the general public. The project was launched at Customs House in Sydney on February 10th, 1999. This prestigious venue at Circular Quay, only recently opened to showcase contemporary craft, was provided free of charge in support of the project. In a long gallery bounded on one side by a sandstone wall and lit on the other by a five storey high atrium, the first group of 21 donated quilts was displayed to great acclaim.

The Honourable Henry Tsang OAM, MLC, then Deputy Lord Mayor of Sydney, and now Member of the Legislative Council of New South Wales launched the project in an enthusiastic speech. He subsequently became the patron of QUILTS 2000. With the assistance of Paralympian Donna Ritchie, Australian wheelchair basketball champion,

Mr Tsang unveiled *The Lizzie Quilt*, the project's logo quilt, and was the first to enter a bid for it. Eileen Campbell, a prominent Melbourne quiltmaker, had been commissioned to make the piece. It features the Paralympic mascot Lizzie, a frill-necked lizard, running from Kakadu down to Sydney for the Games. *The Lizzie Quilt* has since become a familiar and much-loved sight in magazines and exhibitions around Australia.

Exhibitions were organised in a range of venues, from small country halls to The Australian Women's Weekly Craft Show in several state capitals. By the conclusion of the project, there were more than fifty exhibitions of the quilts around Australia. The quilts also travelled to New Zealand and Japan giving hundreds of thousands of people the opportunity to see the quilts and hear about the Paralympic Games.

Many donations arrived through the post. Others were hand delivered at exhibitions, giving committee members and quiltmakers an opportunity to meet. The stories that

Henry Tsang, Eileen Campbell, Donna Ritchie, Dianne Finnegan, Margaret Wright and Lois Appleby, CEO of SPOC, at the launch

Hamish Mac Donald matches his hand to *Our Helping Hands* (108) by the children of Temora West Public School I.O. class

surround the making of the quilts were inspirational. Some quiltmakers drove for hours to attend shows. Rosemary Small, a teacher from Temora Primary School, arrived at The Australian Women's Weekly Craft Show in Melbourne with her husband and son. They had driven for five hours so she could present the quilt, *Our Helping Hands* (108, p143). Made by a group of disabled children, each had chosen a Paralympic athlete to honour in a block, with a hand print and their names in the quilt. Recognition of their work in the national media gave the children a great sense of achievement.

During the quilt gathering phase, letters, emails and telephone calls to the committee brought word of the special efforts that people were putting into their quilts and their particular reasons for involvement. The maker might have a relation or friend who was disabled and the quilt was made to honour that person. Patricia Rolfe's son, David, is one of Australia's elite athletes with a disability who is currently enjoying great success in his chosen field of swimming. Patricia donated *Good Neighbourhood* (127, p145), in recognition of this success.

Sometimes, the completion of the quilt required a huge effort under difficult conditions, but the deadline was met. Perhaps the handing over of the quilt was part of a healing process—a sense of achievement gained from helping others. Yvonne Williams made *Go Neville* (530, p38) to honour Neville Barnes, a wheelchair athlete and basketballer who represented Australia in Japan and England in the 1980's. Neville had been a close friend of the family who often shared his expertise in farming.

Each contributor was offered a press kit to provide to the local media to publicise the project, and the resulting articles and television coverage forged further links. Janet Shepherd explained to a journalist that her quilt, *Advancing Together* (76, p. 40), had been made to honour the man in a wheelchair who practised up and down on the footpath in front of her house. The enterprising journalist waited outside for Ronald Gibson and invited him in to meet the quiltmaker. A new friendship was formed.

Athletes training for the Paralympic Games volunteered their time to speak at many exhibition openings. Their matter-of-fact accounts of gruelling training schedules and the glory of past achievements served to spur many quiltmakers on to greater efforts for the cause. At the launch, Donna Ritchie had the audience in stitches, when she described her aversion to needlework classes at primary school. The experience convinced her she would need to excel in sport to escape making quilts!

The quilts ventured further into the community through the efforts of individuals and guilds. June Brown included a selection of the quilts at the Wangarratta Textile Festival in Victoria. Subsequently the Wangaratta Centre Quilters purchased Beth Roberts'

Go Australia, Go! (286, p71) and presented it to the local Council to hang in the Civic Centre. She also donated her award-winning quilt, *After the Rain* (49, p92). This was one of several donated quilts that had previously been awarded prizes.

Lee White also handed over her quilt, *Australian Kookaburra* (105, p51) in Melbourne—it was one of the first to sell. An earlier quilt by Lee had been presented to the Atlanta Organising Committee of the Olympic Games from the Sydney Organising Committee.

Some local councils in New South Wales were supporters of the Sydney 2000 Paralympic Games and as a visible token of this support, many provided free venues and assistance for the display of the quilts. Blacktown City Council was particularly supportive and was the first to make a major purchase, acquiring Penelope Neil's quilt, *Rejoice in Australia* (117, p69). Shoalhaven Council soon followed, purchasing a locally-made quilt (320, p74). Councils with regional art galleries waived fees to hang quilts in these prestigious settings. Camden Council was particularly supportive; 200 quilts were displayed at the Civic Centre. A record 17 quilts sold from the exhibition, one being acquired by the council, *Natural Power* by The Epping Quilters (190, p101).

Major companies also expressed their support for the Paralympics by acquiring quilts. Brother International (Australasia) acquired Jenny Bowker's quilt, *Spring in the Sunburnt Country* (81, p73). The health fund, MBF, chose five quilts for display in their foyers across Australia (70, p72; 239, p105; 249, p138; 284, p80 and 264, p114). Management Performance Systems acquired two quilts, *Mola* (35, p150) and *Paralympians are all Stars* (87, p139) as did Ronald Tapp Holdings (99, p134).

Blacktown City Council's new acquisition, *Rejoice in Australia* (117, p69) by Penelope Neil with General Manager Terry McCormack, Margaret Wright, Dianne Finnegan and Mayor Alan Pendelton.

Professional organisations were also supportive. The Australian Institute of Sport in Canberra mounted a display of quilts in the Ansett Visitors' Centre and the main administration building in the year leading up to the Games. More than 80,000 people pass through the Visitors' Centre annually, so these vibrant expressions of the Australian landscape and culture had incredible exposure in a sporting environment. On a much shorter time-scale, there was a small exhibition of quilts at the Adelaide conference of the Australasian College of Physicians in May 2000. Jenny Loss' quilt, *Australian Flora* (93, p98) was purchased by Rosemary Penman from the College.

At the instigation of Helen Beck of Makers Mark, the quilts were displayed in their Melbourne retail outlet and in the foyer of the office block at 101 Collins Street, Melbourne. These two prestigious locations exposed the quilts to the 'top end of town' and provided excellent selling opportunities.

Mary Clarke, of SPOC, helped to ensure that QUILTS 2000 was represented at events organised by other Paralympic sponsors and supporters. The Business Club at St Andrews Cathedral School in Sydney auctioned a quilt at its fund raising black tie dinner for two consecutive years. Seniors Card successfully bid for *The Lost Wave* by Christa Sanders (39, p56) and provided any practical assistance they could.

A selection of quilts was displayed in the foyer of Parliament House in Sydney, marking the One Year To Go celebrations. At a function at the same venue, politicians gathered to hear Premier Bob Carr endorse the Paralympic Games and the QUILTS 2000 project. In April 2000, the quilts were shown at Parliament House in Canberra, the seat of the

The Foyer of 101 Collins Street, Melbourne, March, 2000

Federal Government. Three quilts were acquired for the permanent collection of the House: *Kangaroo Feathers* by Beth Reid (90, p64), *Waves Over the Inland Sea* by Christine Hawker (502, 56) and *Irish Chain* by Andra Swan (564, 126)

From the time of the launch, there was also a 'virtual exhibition' on the QUILTS 2000 website, www.Quilts2000.org.au. Quiltmakers could access the quilt gallery, find their own quilt and read about the project. Potential buyers had instant access to pictures of the quilts. Prior to the QUILTS 2000 website, the biggest show could only display as many as 200 quilts, but with this technology, the entire collection could be available on the web continuously. To enhance the images, the quilts were all photographed digitally by Andrew Payne of Photographix, an herculean task organised by Karen Fail. Having the quilt photographs in digital form made it much easier to provide high-quality images for publicity purposes and for selling opportunities.

In the midst of these exhibitions, three other opportunities arose. PINWORX, a company making pins for the Sydney 2000 Olympic and Paralympic Games, offered to make a pin for QUILTS 2000 featuring a quilt, the project logo and the Sydney Paralympic torch logo. Jane Gibson's quilt, *Flaming Stars* (34, p111) was chosen for its strong, graphic qualities. The pins were sold to raise funds and were also presented to important people involved in different stages of the project. So, for instance, a Paralympian speaking at the opening of an exhibition, would be presented with a pin as a memento. Many people who could not buy a quilt, were happy to buy a pin. Following the success of this pin, a new one was released based on *Magpies and Wattle* by Queanbeyan Quilters (238, p105). Everyone wore the pins as a constant promotion of the project.

QUILTS 2000 pin 1

QUILTS 2000 pin 2

Jane Gibson (left) talking to a visitor to The Australian Women's Weekly Craft Fair in Brisbane about her quilt *Flaming Stars* (34 p111) on which the first QUILTS 2000 pin was modelled.

Rowan Kelly of the Real Estate
Institute auctions Alysoun Ryves'
500 Days to Go (611, p153))

PINWORX was also producing pins for each significant date leading up to the Games. Each pin celebrated one of the eighteen sports in the Paralympic Games. Quiltmakers were invited to make a quilt for every milestone, *500 Days To Go, 400 Days To Go* etcetera, featuring the appropriate sport. Each of these quilts had to incorporate several images provided to the quiltmaker: the Sydney Paralympic logo, the QUILTS 2000 logo, an image of Lizzie as an athlete in appropriate sport mode, and the number of days to go to the launch of the Games. Each quilt design had to be approved by the Sydney Paralympic Organising Committee. Volunteers to make these quilts were called for and several of the country's top quiltmakers were approached. In all, eighteen quilts were made in this series. Each was presented and sold throughout the project. The Real Estate Institute (REI), a supporter of the Sydney Paralympic Games, was particularly helpful, providing experienced auctioneers to conduct some auctions. The first quilt, *500 Days to Days* (611, p153) featured the sport of archery and was made by Alysoun Ryves. It was auctioned in The Rocks by Rowan Kelly, Vice President of the Institute. The Northern Beaches Christmas meeting of the REI provided the venue for the auction of the *300 Days To Go* quilt, made by Larraine Scouler (613, p152).

Other opportunities arose as word of the project spread. Two other supporters of the Sydney 2000 Paralympic Games commissioned quilts. Seniors Card asked for a quilt featuring their 'Million Smiles' fundraising campaign and were delighted with Jane Gibson's quilt, *A Million Smiles,* (65, p120). The World Forest 2000 Foundation commissioned Julie Woods' quilt, *Evergreen*, (479, p67), showcasing their environmental concerns. Sailability, the organisation supporting Paralympic sailing, also commissioned a quilt, Dale Brown's *Sydney Mosaic* (603, p116).

Detail of *Evergreen* (479, p67)
commissioned by World Forest
2000, made by Julie Woods

The deadline for the receipt of quilts was late January 2000. The quilts could then be photographed, the images loaded onto the website and the sale of the Collection launched. With the quilts gathered briefly for photography, it was also an opportunity to judge them. As part of its sponsorship, Brother International (Australasia) had provided three prizes for the quiltmakers: $5000 to an individual quiltmaker and $2000 to a group whose quilt best captured the spirit of Australia or were the best expression of the Paralympic ideals. All quiltmakers were entered into a draw to win the third prize—a top-of-the-line Brother sewing machine.

Judy Hooworth, well-known quilt artist and author; Christina Sumner, Curator of Decorative Arts at the Museum of Applied Arts and Sciences, Sydney; and Dianne Finnegan, quilt artist, international lecturer, author and a committee member of QUILTS 2000, were the judges. The major individual prizewinner was Christa Sanders from Spence, ACT for her quilt, *World Games, Circles of Endurance, Sydney 2000* (22, p35), portraying in coloured circles, the journey of an athlete through passion and dark times on to gold. The group quilt, *Flames of Glory* (291, p34), made by The Possum Patchers, Mundaring, WA, is an exuberant celebration of achievement. The colourwash quilt comes together seamlessly—a considerable achievement for a quilt worked on by many hands. Forty-seven QUILTS 2000 Awards were given to quilts commended by the judges.

After the quilts were received, the selling phase could begin. The Mayor of the Paralympic Village and retiring Deputy Prime Minister, Tim Fischer, launched the Collection and this phase, supported by Deputy Mayors Sarina Bratton and Peter Trotter. Held at SPOC headquarters, the event was well attended by press and dignitaries as well as several makers of the quilts on display.

Sue Ellen Lovett was the guest of honour, accompanied by her guide dog Eccles. This famous equestrian had made two marathon rides to raise funds for the Paralympics: from

Judges (l to r) Dianne Finnegan, Judy Hooworth and Christina Sumner

Lois Appleby, CEO of SPOC, Tim Fischer, Mayor of the Paralympics Village and Deputy Mayors Sarina Bratton and Peter Trotter at the launch of the sale of the Collection at SPOC headquarters

Sue Ellen Lovett with her guide dog Eccles enjoys the quilt (254, p55) honouring her fundraising ride from Brisbane to Sydney

Judith Burgess (in white) with Annette Baggie, John Butler and Ann Jones of The Galahs at the launch of the Collection

Nancye Donaldson and Del Patterson with their quilt honouring Grant Hackett (309, p37)

Melbourne to Sydney and from Brisbane to Sydney. The latter journey was celebrated in the quilt, *Somewhere Along the Way* (254, p55), made by Lorraine Smith.

This quilt provided the backdrop for the speeches by Margaret Wright, Lois Appleby and Tim Fischer. The quilt had already been sold on its first showing at a Businessmen's Breakfast organised by Manly Council.

Among the quiltmakers present to witness the unveiling of their quilts were Annette Baggie and Anne Jones, representing their group The Galahs. They were pleased to meet John Butler, whose painting had inspired their quilt *Gathering of Friends* (36, p119). John had also produced drawings for another quilt, *All John's Creatures* by The Butler Birds (631) which were hand embroidered in black thread on homespun and featured Australian animals and birds. These naive quilts are like picture books with engaging stories of people portrayed as animals.

In his speech, Tim Fischer suggested that organisers of the Olympic and Paralympic Games should have quilts on their walls because of their calming influence. Fischer's suggestion may have been the impetus for three special sales. The Australian Olympic Committee acquired *A Nation United* (309, p37), featuring swimmer Grant Hackett. Del Patterson, who painted the image of the swimmer, and quiltmaker Nancye Donaldson both attended the launch. The purchase was a great gesture of support for the Paralympics and an exciting image for the Committee's offices. It was doubly significant as this was the only quilt permitted to display the Olympic rings. The International Paralympic Committee (IPC) subsequently acquired two quilts, *Games 2000* by Ruth Knight (246, p144) and *Lizzie's Games* by Mary Osborne (348, p36).

Mary-Anne Danaher, Craft Editor of *The Australian Women's Weekly* came up with the selling slogan: 'Be a sport … Buy a quilt!' This was featured on the brochure which was printed by Diamond Press, a Supporter of the

Paralympic Games. The brochure has proved invaluable for spreading awareness of the quilt selling program.

Quilt buyers identified closely with the project. These quilts are unlike store-bought memorabilia—they are the gift of Australian quiltmakers to the world, and buyers recognise this. Sales forms often came with messages of support and thanks for the opportunity to be a part of the project. These were sometimes followed up by telephone calls. Researching an article on 'Collecting' for *The Sydney Morning Herald*, journalist Judy Adamson was so captivated by the quilts that she immediately bought one on the website, even though this was her first contact with quilts. In a later telephone interview with Margaret Wright, she expressed her admiration for the project and the quilts.

By having quilts for sale on the Internet, international sales became possible. There was a great buzz when an order came from afar, whether it was from the United States, Germany, or the other side of Australia. One order for five quilts came from Western Australia, while a woman from the United States bought seven quilts. It set us thinking—had someone bought pieces for a whole family or had they organised a group of friends to buy in one order? One quiltmaker, aware that many of her friends did not have access to the Internet and were not computer literate, organised an 'Internet café'. She provided morning tea in her home and showed the group how to navigate around the website!

The ability to communicate globally, the scope of information available to the public and the speed with which information could be disseminated, all added to the success of the website, bringing national and international sales daily.

The grand finale of the project had not occurred at the time of writing. All the quilts are to be at Sydney Olympic Park from October 19th to the 29th as part of the Sydney 2000 Paralympic Games Arts Festival, under the direction of Leo Schofield. It is destined to be the one of the biggest and the best quilt shows ever in Australia. Some of the outstanding quilts have been chosen as the feature decor of the Athletes' Village to be seen by international media, National Organising Committees and by athletes throughout the Olympics and Paralympics.

After the Paralympic Games are over, the quilts will be forwarded to their new owners, the project complete. This book has been created to preserve the memory of the project, the quilts and the people. The National Library also appreciated the significance of the project as a document of social history, and archived the website in its Electronic Unit as part of its Pandora (Preserving and Accessing Networked Documentary Resources of Australia) Archive on their website: *http://pandora.nla.gov.au/pandora/*

All John's Creatures (631) by the Butler Birds. Detail of work in progress. Hand embroidered animals and flowers.

One of John Butler's paintings reproduced in the quilt.

Each committee member brought her own special skills to the project — promotion, exhibition design, data recording, marketing, networking, writing, web design...

The Team

Margaret Wright

Cathie Bogard

Karen Fail

Dianne Finnegan

Hitomi Fujita

Jane Gibson

Alysoun Ryves

Carolyn Sullivan

Jan T Urquhart

Choy-Lin Williams

Christa Sanders and Judy Turner hand over their quilts to Margaret Wright, March, 1999, at the Australian Women's Weekly Fair in Canberra

The committee of QUILTS 2000 included ten women. Most had been office bearers of their state or regional quilters' guilds. Karen Fail, Dianne Finnegan, Carolyn Sullivan and Margaret Wright had all served terms as president of The Quilters' Guild, the largest guild in Australia. Jan Urquhart had been president of Queensland Quilters. Alysoun Ryves had been president of the Hunters Hill Quilters, while Cathie Bogard, Jane Gibson and Choy-Lin Williams were former committee members of The Quilters' Guild. Hitomi Fujita runs her own related small business.

As chairman, Margaret was the driving force behind the project. The Paralympians' slogan of *'Set No Limits'* certainly applied to her. Margaret was in control of the overall plan, as well as the day-to-day decisions. Her ability always to get things done by impossible deadlines—regardless of the problems involved—was an example to all.

Each committee member brought special skills to the project. Karen, Dianne, Carolyn and Jan had all written quilting books and Jan was formerly editor of *Down Under Quilts*. Choy-Lin had been editor of *The Template*, the magazine of The Quilters' Guild. All had organised quilt exhibitions and had a wide network of friends in the quilting world. These networks proved to be invaluable! When we did not have a skill or lacked the introduction to an important contact, there was always someone who knew someone who could help us. On a site visit to the Athletes' Village while it was under construction, Margaret Wright introduced herself to the site manager only to be met with, 'I know you, we met at the Witchcraft Quilt Show. My wife is a quilter!'

As the need arose, new skills were developed. Karen not only became adept at publicity and handling the media, she devised a marketing plan. In their endeavours to spread the quilts widely, Margaret and Dianne even donned hard hats and steel-capped boots to check out the railway station being constructed under Sydney's International Airport for an exhibition at a Businessmen's Breakfast organised by Kathy Jones of Airport Link. As Margaret had the last two boots available for site visitors, she looked like quite comical—both boots were not only huge, but also different sizes!

Alysoun's organisational skills and fund raising abilities were invaluable, while Jane must have developed muscles as she caught the bus daily to the post office to collect or despatch the latest batch of quilts, to and from all corners of the country. Coordinating with Choy-Lin, who transferred all information to a database, Jane kept track of all the quilts, and seemed to know every one of them intimately. She could quote name, number and title without checking. She only started to falter when the count exceeded five hundred quilts. When commenting on the efficacy of a virtual quilt exhibition on the website, Jane wryly commented that they did not feel like virtual quilts when she was lugging them to and from the post office.

Jan's expertise with designing print layouts gave us 'the look' of the project. With her knowledge of the Internet, she designed the site, *www.Quilts2000.org.au,* which brought the project to the world. Quiltmakers and potential buyers could access the site and be updated on the quilts, exhibitions and other events. Annie Whitsed assisted Jan

Jan Urquhart and Mary-Anne Danaher at the launch, Customs House, Sydney in February, 1999

George Nawa, Brother International (Australasia) and Margaret Wright

The Honourable Bob Carr, MP, Premier of NSW at Parliament House, Sydney

to complete the website. When the sheer volume of quilts became unmanageable for one person, Karen wrote the news pages for the site.

Data recording and handling was achieved so smoothly by Choy-Lin that it appeared effortless to the rest of the group. Information was updated daily and any query speedily answered. Living far from the committee in Nowra, in country New South Wales, Kerry Sutherland directed all incoming email to the appropriate committee member.

Carolyn was in charge of the newsletter to groups and guilds. This was an important vehicle for building interest and spreading awareness of the Paralympics. Everyone who expressed interest in making a quilt was sent early information regarding ticketing for the Paralympic Games.

Cathie was treasurer of the group and kept track of the budget. She oversaw quilt sales with the assistance of Gwenyth Mitchell.

Hitomi Fujita's bilingual capabilities became vital as the project intensified. Our major sponsor, Brother International (Australasia), is a Japanese-based company, so Hitomi was a great help in our communications. She organised articles about the project for Japanese publications and translated them into Japanese. She also wrote for Sydney-based Japanese newspapers and was responsible for mounting an exhibition at the Kai Tea Rooms and Gallery to showcase a selection of the quilts. Hitomi was also the mail clerk for QUILTS 2000.

Roy Adcock hands over the cheque for *500 Days to Go* (611, p153) to Margaret Wright after the auction at PINWORX.
Mary Clarke from SPOC on the right.

Dianne was responsible for developing exhibitions, aided by Alysoun, Margaret and Karen. Margaret, Karen and Dianne formed the executive in charge of operations and were responsible for planning.

Although neither a member of the committee nor even a quiltmaker, the other person essential to the success of the project was Mary Clarke, Senior Marketing Manager, Sydney 2000 Paralympic Organising Committee. Her cheerful 'can do' attitude and professionalism carried us over many hurdles. She put us in touch with other organisations involved in major fundraising projects for the Paralympic Games and these links proved valuable to all.

As a voluntary group with no central office, there was always the problem of distributing and tracking information, quilts, frames and other equipment. Nevertheless, the group came together seamlessly. Everyone assisted in assembling and dismantling exhibitions. Sometimes more than one exhibition occurred in the same week, so this was a major investment of time and effort. Family members and friends were also roped in to help and all gave their time happily. Even Mary Clarke, who was often at openings in her official capacity, volunteered her help beyond the call of duty.

A much larger band were the quiltmakers.

The quiltmakers came from every state in Australia. They represented country areas and cities and even included Australians living overseas. Also represented were quilt groups, embroiderers' groups, textile artists and classes of school children—some of whom had never made a quilt.

QUILTS 2000 was a widespread, grass roots response to the Paralympic Games in Australia. The project capitalised on the groundswell of support for the Paralympians. Quilters 'pumped irons' for the Games and sewed kilometres (miles).

Karen Fail receives *We Are One* (233, p110) from The Robina Crazy Patchworkers at The Australian Womens Weekly Craft Fair in Brisbane, October, 1999

Paul Nanari, Paralympian, opens the Camden exhibition, March 2000

Margaret Wright hands over the first cheque from QUILTS 2000 to Lois Appleby, CEO of SPOC at the launch of the Collection, February, 2000

Karen Fail talks to the Liverpool Quilters, August 1999. During the collection of the quilts, committee members spoke to many groups about the project and encouraged participation.

Sports records are often expressed in figures, so here are a few from the project:

- more than 2,000 people made 630 quilts requiring more than 200,000 hours of voluntary work

- over 600 kilometres (375 miles) of thread were used in the quilting and machine-embroidery

- 3750 running metres (almost 2 miles) of fabric were used in the making of the quilts

- if laid end to end, the quilts would stretch 2½ times around the track of The Olympic Stadium

- committee members spoke about the project at more than 100 speaking engagements

- quilts were exhibited in 56 shows

Other notable records:

- Audrey McMahon was the oldest quiltmaker at ninety years old (578, p78).

- the youngest were Rona Zippora at 11 years and Miriam Solomon at 10 years of age (395, p52).

Quiltmakers have always been known for their generosity. This project was no exception, but had the added dimension of sport, bringing many new faces with it. Awareness of the Olympic Games and the Paralympic Games increased dramatically during the project, which also helped communicate our message.

The QUILTS 2000 project succeeded because of the people involved. Go, the quilters!

Margaret Wright, Hitomi Fujita, Dianne Finnegan and Karen Fail at the Boondall Craft Fair, Brisbane, April, 1999

Jane Gibson inspecting and labelling quilts as they arrive

Alysoun Ryves with a stack of quilts gathered in her home for Awards Day

Margaret Wright, Judy Hooworth and Choy-Lin Williams contemplate some of the quilts on Awards Day, February, 2000

The collection forms

a joyful, vibrant record

of the Australian way

of life. The diversity

of images, colours and

styles gives a truly

kaleidoscopic view.

The QUILTS 2000 collection encompasses multiple visions of Australia. The quilts provide a survey of Australian life and landscape (both urban and country), matters of current concern, and the preoccupation with sport, ideals and aspirations of sports people. The collection forms a joyful, vibrant record of the Australian way of life. The diversity of images, colours and styles gives a truly kaleidoscopic view.

Installation shot of foyer of the ABC,
Ultimo, February 2000

Quiltmakers were invited to make quilts with an Australian flavour and draw on the diversity of this wide continent—its land, people, native plants and animals—which all make up the 'spirit' of Australia. Alternatively they could express the Paralympic theme. The power, performance and pride of the athletes as they train to attain their pinnacle in competition, suggested the theme of 'P' words as a design source for the quilts. Perfection, purpose, partnership and perseverance were all represented.

To easily hang the quilts in exhibitions and freight them around the country to different venues, guidelines were provided. The quilt must fit within an area no smaller than 90 centimetres (36 inches) square and no larger than 150 centimetres (59 inches) square, with the top edge horizontal and at least as wide as the rest of the quilt. This definition allowed for quilts that were not rectangles, but would hang easily from a top rod. Some quiltmakers took advantage of the opportunity to make uneven-sided quilts within these constraints (for example 438, p36, and 400, p144). Because the quilts might be folded for transportation to exhibitions, they could not be rigid, nor have loose or delicate surface embellishment.

Quiltmakers used the quilt surface as a canvas, so they can also be read as a form of cultural text. Some of the quilts take this more literally by incorporating text in their design. The 'P' words figure prominently in some (for example, 96, p128, and 183, p38), while others incorporated sayings, such as 'A Few Kangaroos Loose in the Top Paddock', which is also the title of the quilt (281, p62).

The Australian larrikin sense of humour is evident in many of the quilts. Apart from the loose kangaroos, one quilt composed of handkerchiefs is titled *On the Nose* (216, p120). Another delightful quilt provides much enjoyment with the antics of animals portraying different sports, such as the lyrebird with gymnastic ribbons (400, p144). Judith Burgess's quilt, *Up the Creek* (111, p121), has animals backstroking up a stream under the watchful eye of the timekeeper. Her daughter's comment that the lizard did not have a good technical style raised the issue of whether a lizard had ever

Detail of *Turning Wheels* (96, p128) using 'P' words for the centre motif.

A Few Kangaroos Loose In The Top Paddock (281, p62)

Detail of backstroke training in *Up the Creek* by Judith Burgess,

Detail off flags spelling out 'Sydney 2000' (503, p117)

Opera House in Mariner's Harbour (detail 64, p116)

Centre star of Adina Sullivan's *Under Aussie Stars* (detail 235, 79)

Overlay of stars in Epping Quilters' *National Pride* (detail 189, p 101))

backstroked! This is one of many quilts that is unashamedly jingoistic. *Echidna* (239, p105), by Frances Mulholland, is another fun image.

The Opera House and harbour are inseparable images of Sydney, so there are several quilts featuring them, such as Sue Wademan's *Sydney Harbour—The Spirit of Sydney* (107, p133). The Opera House also features in Lyndall Pickering's *Mariners' Harbour* (64, p116). Cecily Dunstall's quilt, *Reflections of the Sydney Opera House* (405, p57), portrays music and an Australian icon.

Sailing, introduced as a Paralympic sport for the first time in 2000, is represented in several quilts. Evelyn Pepper's quilt, *Reaching Towards Sydney* 2000 (503, p117), uses flags to represent the words 'Sydney 2000'.

Stars are another recurrent theme. The Southern Cross on the Australian flag, glows from several quilts, but stars are also a recognition of the universality of the event, they figure prominently on many national flags. Adina Sullivan's quilt, *Under Aussie Skies* (235, p79), is an original arrangement of a traditional pattern. The moon and the sun also featured on the quilts: Choy-Lin Williams' *The Calm Before ...* (7, p151) was a very popular quilt and Dianne Firth's *Blaze* (26, p103) glows with inner light.

Another image to emerge as a favourite was the heart. Perhaps because the heart represents caring, quiltmakers were drawn to it to express their support of the Paralympians. Pam Bellamy's quilt, *Hearts Delight* (274, p122), is a typical example.

A major preoccupation in Australian painting is the landscape, so it is not surprising that the same theme was so popular in the quilts. Gloria Loughman's *Spirit of Kata Tjuta* (272, p65) uses hand dyed fabrics to bring the barren landscape of Central Australia to life. Cynthia Morgan's quilt, *Window on Murchison* (1, p107), has a great sense of depth, looking through a jagged hole in a rocky escarpment at the river beyond.

The format of block quilts was often used to capture a wide variety of subjects, from farm scenes (267 and 383, pp144, 120), to native flowers (104 and 268, pp124, 124) and animals (127 and 382, pp145, 44). In *National Pride* (189, p101) and *Natural Power* (190, p101), the Epping Quilters obscure the block structure with an overlay of the Southern Cross. The former portrays achievements in rural life, mining and community activities, while the latter is concerned with fellowship in times of disaster.

Makers have progressed beyond reproducing patterns directly from books. The quilts that are based on traditional repeat block patterns have been chosen by their makers for their appropriateness and coloured with reference to the country. The Novocastrian Quilters gave the popular Log Cabin design an Australian feel by their choice of colour in *Tracks Around a Sunburnt Country* (144, p134). The concentric squares call to mind the graphic nature of Aboriginal art.

The combination of tradition and original design with a contemporary reference is well illustrated by Ann Haddad's quilt, *Oz Gold* (264, p114). She takes the format of a geometric repeat block, but arranges the blocks into a diamond and adds an original block she designed based on the Paralympic torch.

Oz Gold (detail 264, p114)

Predictably, Australian animals, birds and flowers featured frequently, but other themes also emerged. Maps of Australia were represented in many quilts, in various styles and techniques. Penelope Neil's *Rejoice in Australia* (117, p69) has exquisitely appliquéd birds, animals, flowers, landforms, icons and other images adorning the map. Very different in style and technique is *An Ancient Land* (494, p122) by Susan Creek and Patricia Hull, an apparently haphazardly pieced rendition of the map in recycled denim, assembled in the Australian tradition of 'making do'.

Animals nestling within the map of Penelope Neil's *Rejoice in Australia* (detail 117, p 69)

Lorraine Banck used the map in an original manner by portraying it as the medal on the end of the ribbon tying together native flowers in a bouquet for the winner. Her quilt, *Dreams Fulfilled* (283, p134), was acquired by Lois Appleby for her office at SPOC headquarters. In *Waves Over the Inland Sea* (502, p56), Christine Hawker addressed a common complaint of Tasmanians: that they are often ignored—she suspended an extra block from the bottom right-hand corner of her quilt.

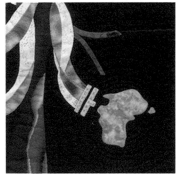

Map swinging from a bouquet in Lorraine Banck's *Dreams Fulfilled* (detail 283, p134)

Representations of Paralympians and Olympic athletes were very powerful. *Good On You Lucy* (84, p45), by Lynda Hannam, celebrated the efforts of Lucy Williams, who has cerebral palsy and trained in the Paralympic Preparation Programme. The quilt was acquired by Lucy's local community to present to her in recognition of her achievements. *The Basketballer* (42, p36), with a wheelchair basketballer shooting a goal is one of a pair of quilts made by the Verandah Post Patchworkers. In a guesture of support, this quilt was acquired by the Braidwood Quilters who also donated a quilt. Pat Finn's quilt, *Going for Gold* (2, p41), shows many sports people silhouetted within an exciting combination of traditional pieced patterns.

The use of silhouettes was a device employed by several quiltmakers. Diana Vincent's *Wild Rhythms* (120, p118) and Susan Lancaster's *From the Outback to the Reef* (60, p108) are just two examples.

Denim patchwork of Australia in *An Ancient Land* (494, p122) by Susan Creek and Patricia Hull

There were a few quilts with an Aboriginal design influence. Jenny Searle's *Childhood Dreaming* (131, p93) and Dianne Finnegan's *Ripples* (12, p99) both reflect the impact of Aboriginal design concepts.

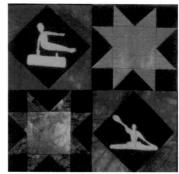

Silhouettes of athletes in Pat Finn's *Going for Gold* (2, p41)

Aboriginal fabric features in Pam Slater's *Bush Tucker* (170 p90)

Raw edge strips woven in *Summer Days* by Beth Reid (91 p58)

Y2K computer bug in Dijanne Cevaal's *Millennium Bug* (156 p85)

In Aboriginal art and in the quilts, handprints are a recurring image—they not only conjure up painted images on rock walls, but are common to all countries. Five of the quilts donated by The Champagne Quilters are covered in handprints (540—544, p150). The Temora West Public School I.O. Class quilt (108, p143) has already been mentioned.

Drawing on the Australian tradition of using superceded tailors' samples, a number of bush quilts in traditional wool rectangles also emerged. Diana Drake's *Pioneer's Rug* (32, p100) is a typical example, Anna Drago's *Posh* (20, p100) upgrades the style by using remnants of expensive fabrics. Barbara Fitton uses the format as a background for Australian flowers in wool embroidery in *Colours of Australia* (458, p100)

The fabric choices extended to the use of hand dyed cloth and of locally designed fabrics, featuring Australiana or those designed by Aboriginal artists. For example *Brownies Stitch Australia* by the Berowra Brownies (427, p46) and *Glimpses of Australia* by Isobel Castles (178, p86). Several quilts featured cotton fabric designed by indigenous Australians, such as Pam Slater's *Bush Tucker* (170, p90) and Leanne McGill's *Do Your Best No Matter What* (138, p91). These two quilts appear very different, but both use the fabric designs to good effect.

The extensive use of hand dyed cloth allows the exact colours and textured effects sought by the maker. For Suzie Cheel, a textile artist who specialises in dyeing silks and creating garments, making a quilt for QUILTS 2000 was a new direction for her work. She found the exercise energising and looks forward to exploring this medium further. Suzie used her own hand dyed silks to piece together *Colourscape* (122, p83).

Colour studies, based on different aspects of the country, were represented in many quilts. Some were traditional patterns with Australian colours, such as Jane Wilson's *Oz Flower Pinwheels* (236, p130); others were entirely original, such as Beth Reid's *Summer Days* (91, p58) and *Inland Haze* (92, p90), with the raw edged strips woven together.

Bushfires obviously play an important part in the national psyche. Barbara Macey's quilt, *Hot North Wind* (440, p109), using subtle variations of red, has a sense of swirling movement and scorching heat. Alison Schwabe's *Bushfire Weather* (47, p97) conjures up a very different environment—the orange, brown and red of the earth and the crack of lightning.

Many of the quilts are more narrative than in the past, when abstract geometric blocks were most popular, so the quilts better tell the stories of our time. Dijanne Cevaal's *Millennium Bug* (156, p85) takes a humorous look at the impact on computers of the dawn of the new millennium. Alison Muir's *Reflections of a Saline Land* (89, p49) is a stark reminder of environmental degradation, something to be addressed in these times of the 'Green Games'.

Immaculate hand work was evident in many quilts. Narelle Grieve's *Paralympians Are All Stars* (87, p139) is one of several hand quilted wholecloth quilts. It has a Mariner's Compass, stars, and the title message worked in cording. Machine and hand embroidery were used extensively throughout the collection.

Beth Roberts' quilt, *Go, Australia, Go!* (286, p71), sums up the spirit of the project. With its Greek Key border and emblematic athletes, it recalls the origins of the Games. Lizzie, mascot of the Sydney 2000 Paralympic Games leads the athletes in their race. As the 2004 Games are in Athens, the quilt not only looks back, but looks forward to Sydney and Athens in its imagery. Machine embroidered fireworks illuminating the Sydney skyline express the sense of celebration in this the beginning of the new millenium.

Athletes, the land, the Sydney skyline, excitement; all these elements run through the QUILTS 2000 collection.

Fireworks over the Sydney skyline in detail of Beth Roberts' *Go, Australia, Go!* (286, p 71)

Enjoy the quilts for their aesthetic appeal, their technical excellence and their association with the Games

All the quilts completed in time for publication are pictured in the gallery. The huge numbers precluded the possibility of providing a page for each quilt.

Sixty two of the quilts are showcased, their extended captions give an insight into the source of inspiration, the design process, construction and the maker.

Alternate pages show groups of quilts. With such a vast collection it was possible to group quilts on a page by theme, by colour, by shape. So there are pages of quilts on sport, one with hearts, others with block quilts built from individual images, snapshots of animals, flowers, buildings and scenery. Many pages have groupings of quilts based on traditional patterns. Some pages are mixed for variety.

All quilts are numbered; to find details, look up the quilt number in the back of the book in the index by quilt number. Quilts have been indexed by the name of the quiltmaker.

Enjoy the quilts for their aestheic appeal, their technical excellence and their association with the Games. The stories of their making are an evocation of the gift from maker to athlete.

Awards
Individual winner Christa Sanders (22, p35)
Group winner   Possum Patchers (291, p34)

Award certificates
Quilts are marked by † in the Gallery

Individual (by Quilt Number)
2 6 8 26 38 81 84 87 89 93
105 107 111 117 122 138
235 239 250 264 272 283
369
405 422 440 484
503 505 530 561 570

Group (by Quilt Number)
65
108 189
233
322 361 367
400 448 474 478 494
526

15 THE LIZZIE QUILT
100 CM X 150 CM (40 IN X 60 IN)
BY EILEEN CAMPBELL, KEW, VICTORIA
MACHINE APPLIQUED, MACHINE EMBROIDERED, MACHINE QUILTED; COTTON

The Lizzie Quilt is the mascot quilt for QUILTS 2000. Commissioned by QUILTS 2000, this quilt captures the spirit of the events of the year 2000 as Lizzie, the mascot of the Sydney 2000 Paralympic Games, heads across the Australian desert with an impish grin on her face, ready to promote the Games to the world. The Australian floral emblem, golden wattle, decorates the side borders.

The quilt is entirely machine made. Eileen has added a little padding to the largest Lizzie to make it appear as though she is running off the quilt. The wattle blossoms are each made separately, by stitching across holes in fabric like the spokes of a bicycle wheel. Decorative braid is used extensively to outline sections of the quilt.

Eileen is an internationally acclaimed quilt artist, tutor and author whose work has won major awards in quilt shows all over Australia, including Best of Show in Sydney and Melbourne. Her work has been exhibited internationally and she has taught in New Zealand, the United States and Japan, where she tutored at World Quilt Expo in 1998. Eileen has written two books, *Applique Applied* and *U is for Unicorn*.

291 FLAMES OF GLORY
115 CM X 145 CM (46 IN X 58 IN)
BY THE POSSUM PATCHERS, MUNDARING, WESTERN AUSTRALIA
COLOURWASH, FOUNDATION PIECED, HAND QUILTED; COTTON

On the outskirts of Perth, five quiltmakers meet weekly to sew and share their lives. Four of the group met more than seventeen years ago at a local learning centre while their toddlers were minded in the creche, and later worked together for the local school their children attended. The school's emblem is a possum—hence the group's name, the Possum Patchers.

Flames of Glory is their first group quilt. After intense discussion over several weeks, they decided to feature a figure rising out of flames using colourwash techniques. One of the group lay down with her arms outstretched, while the others drew her outline onto a sheet. Armed with 6.5 cm (2fi in) squares cut from their fabric stashes, the group members began filling in the design. To begin, they had prepared A4 sheets of 5 cm (2 in) coded grid that matched the code on the backing sheet onto which the squares were pinned. Each member took two or three 'pages' home each week, and used foundation piecing to complete the blocks, ready for assembly. They all shared in hand quilting the quilt.

Flames of Glory was awarded $2000 for the best quilt made by a group in the QUILTS 2000 collection. This award was funded by Brother International (Australasia), the major sponsor for QUILTS 2000.

22 WORLD GAMES, CIRCLES OF ENDURANCE, SYDNEY 2000
144 CM X 128 CM (57 IN X 51 IN)
BY CHRISTA SANDERS, SPENCE, AUSTRALIAN CAPITAL TERRITORY
MACHINE PIECED AND HAND QUILTED; COTTON

While the journey of any elite athlete is not easy, Paralympians face an added challenge. Their effort is like a never-ending circle, with strength sought from within to face each new obstacle. These constant challenges must often seem like huge mountains to the athletes.

Christa captures her thoughts in her quilt with the red circle representing the passion every individual has for his or her sport and the green circle its constant renewal during all the ups and downs of training and competition. Without a doubt, every athlete encounters the dark side of a steep mountain, the black circle. It is then that the individual looks within for the power and perseverance needed to continue. Every Paralympian in Sydney reaches the gold circle, captured for all time in the blue circle.

Christa Sanders has been making quilts for twenty years and has participated in many solo and group exhibitions. Her work is represented in many significant public and private collections in Australia and overseas.

World Games, Circles of Endurance, Sydney 2000 was awarded $5000 for the best quilt made by an individual in the QUILTS 2000 collection. This award was funded by Brother International (Australasia), the major sponsor for QUILTS 2000.

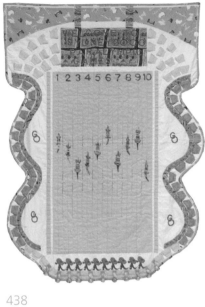

438

42

43

555

433

348

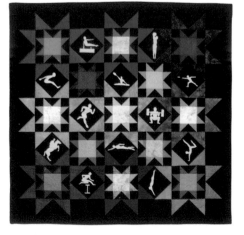

572

347

309 A NATION UNITED
97 CM X 110 CM (38 IN X 44 IN)
BY NANCYE DONALDSON AND DEL PATTERSON, ST. IVES, NEW SOUTH WALES
HAND PAINTED AND FREE MACHINE QUILTED; COTTON, PLASTIC

The image of swimmer, Grant Hackett rising from the water was Nancye's choice to best epitomise the Paralympic themes of power, performance and pride. With permission to use the Olympic rings on her quilt, she contacted Del Patterson to work on the design with her and make the quilt a joint project. Del's powerful painting of Hackett captures the surge in national pride as Australia approached the 2000 Games. The border of many hands in unity highlights the contribution of both the indigenous people and the European settlers to Australia's nationhood, and is symbolic of the cheering crowds. Grant Hackett provided the finishing touch by signing the border.

Del drew and painted the central figure on cotton fabric (previously tea-dyed by Nancye to get a good flesh colour). Together they settled the figure into the carefully chosen 'water' fabric, overlaying the lower part with strips of the background fabric. The figure was lightly padded and Nancye added her unique 'froth and bubble' technique using cellophane.

Nancye is an avid quiltmaker and embroiderer, and a popular tutor. She exhibits regularly at galleries, including the Hotel Gallery, Uluru. Del Patterson is a commercial artist who shows her work in numerous exhibitions and galleries, and is represented in several private collections nationally. In 1991, Nancye and Del mounted an exhibition tilted 'Silk Watercolours and Thread Painting'.

183

† 530

† 478

198

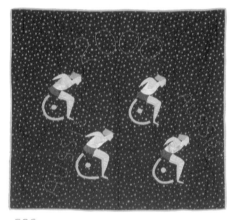

586

465

496

599

523

384 GREEN AND GOLD FOR GLORY
143 cm x 95 cm (57 in x 38 in)
By Carol Heath, Ballarat, Victoria
Machine pieced, machine and hand quilted, photo transfer onto cotton, couched ribbon, beads

When Steve Moneghetti crosses the finishing line first, all Australians cheer. Carol captures the moment in her quilt, with a photo-transferred image of Moneghetti by photographer Tony Feder, official IOC photographer. The two side sections represent the excitement generated by the Sydney 2000 Olympic and Paralympic Games, complete with streamers, against the backdrop of the ancient red land. As a final touch, Carol has included a personal message from Steve Moneghetti to the Sydney 2000 Paralympians: 'Going for glory Paralympians 2000. With my best wishes, Steve Moneghetti'.

Carol has used photo-transfer techniques on a large scale, segmenting and enlarging the original image twice. The final image, made up of sixteen pieces joined, is reminiscent of the large screen used in the Olympic Stadium.

Quilt artist Carol Heath has exhibited widely, including the Russian Cultural Exchange Exhibition in 1998-9 and Quilts From Down Under exhibition in Canada in 1998. She works as a consultant, designer and artist-in-residence for special textile projects, and is a freelance writer specialising in quilt-related articles.

25

590

588

188

413

76

† 2 GOING FOR GOLD

130 CM X 130 CM (52 IN X 52 IN)

BY PAT FINN, CALOUNDRA, QUEENSLAND

MACHINE PIECED, MACHINE APPLIQUED AND MACHINE QUILTED; COTTON, SOME HAND DYED

Combining brilliant colours and innovative settings using traditional patchwork blocks have become standard procedure for Pat Finn. These design elements come together beautifully in *Going for Gold*, a celebration quilt for the Sydney 2000 Games.

Pat has used her hand dyed fabrics to make the traditional blocks, Sawtooth Star and Square in a Square. These are combined with appliqued sporting images to create a quilt which pays tribute to Australia's Olympic and Paralympic sporting stars.

Pat enjoys making art quilts and bed quilts and has done since her daughter gave her two cushion kits in 1986. She uses innovative design and fabrics as she experiments with new directions in her work. While many of her quilts have an original contemporary look, they are often based on traditional patchwork designs. Pat has exhibited her work in New South Wales and Queensland in the hope that others will be inspired to take up the art of quiltmaking.

193

229

269

288

37

350

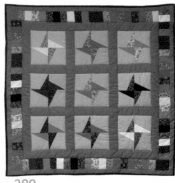

289

489

539

506

† 369 BREAKING BARRIERS
96 CM X 125 CM (38 IN X 50 IN)
BY JANE KINGSTON, AVALON, NEW SOUTH WALES
HAND REVERSE APPLIQUED, MACHINE QUILTED AND TIED; HAND DYED AND PAINTED COTTON

Inspired by the silhouette of a female running, Jane added the Southern Cross to an image in reverse applique. The vision of a runner cutting through the barriers of fatigue is a powerful one, as Jane seeks to pay homage to the outstanding performance and perseverance of Australia's Paralympians.

The design completed, Jane enlarged it using an epidiascope to produce a full-sized pattern. As she cut away the top layer, she revealed the athlete beneath the background fabric, coloured with her specially hand dyed fabric. The background is echo-quilted, with the central figure and stars tied.

Jane was taught to sew from an early age and was always making things. Later, the making of clothes and household items became an economic imperative. Now a medical practitioner, Jane creates for pleasure and relaxation, more recently teaching herself many quilting techniques. Jane's work has won awards in the Sydney Quilt Show in 1998 and 1999 in the Theme Category.

353

566

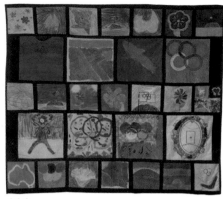

114

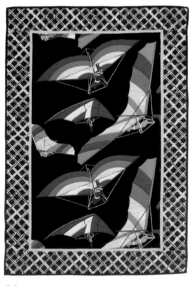

80

394

163

382

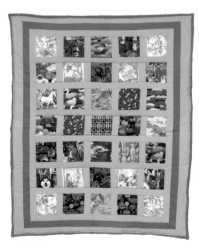

567

371

† 84 GOOD ON YOU LUCY
90 CM X 116 CM (36 IN X 46 IN)
BY LYNDA HANNAM, NEWPORT, NEW SOUTH WALES
MACHINE PIECED AND QUILTED; COTTON

Lucy Williams is the inspiration for Lynda Hannam's quilt, *Good on You Lucy*. Not allowing herself to be restricted by the attitude of others, Lucy forges ahead in her goal to represent Australia in the swimming at the Sydney 2000 Paralympic Games. Lucy has cerebral palsy, but that has never stopped her from leading a satisfying life with her very supportive family. In February 2000, she learned that she was part of the final training squad for the Games.

Making *Good On You Lucy* forced Lynda to experiment and take a different direction from her usual traditional quiltmaking. Although she has always encouraged her students to break the rules and step outside the normal when using colour, it was quite a change for her to use her machine and to cut things up after they were sewn. Her students and her artist son, Edward, assisted her in overcoming design hurdles and a lack of technical know-how.

Support of Lucy has always been important to the Northern Beaches community who sponsored Lucy's first trip overseas to compete. With money raised by the community, *Good On You Lucy* was purchased by her swimming group, the Sea Pirates as a gift to Lucy.

336

71

175

95

184

427

126

160

159

† **448 AUSTRALIA DREAMING**
127 CM X 113 CM (51 IN X 45 IN)
BY THE CENTENARY QUILTERS, WESTLAKE, QUEENSLAND
MACHINE PIECED, HAND APPLIQUED AND HAND QUILTED; COTTON, SOME HAND DYED

The Centenary Quilters are typical of many quilting groups in Australia, who meet regularly to sew, chat and share in the tradition of the quilting bee. Many plans involve raising money for charity or making quilts to give to worthy causes. To meet the challenge of making a quilt for the QUILTS 2000 project, Sally Fletcher, formerly an Australian Army illustrator, designed a stunning Log Cabin quilt with an appliqued procession of athletes.

The colour of each log in the Log Cabin blocks was individually selected and placed on the group's design wall to ensure that everyone was happy with the colours swirling across the quilt. To make the process even more complicated, the blocks were assembled using foundation piecing. Each block was carefully removed from the wall and placed in the right order, ready for piecing at home. In the completed quilt, the images of the athletes are silhouetted against the vibrant log cabins, leading the eye to gold!

Despite this gruelling routine, the group is already organising its next community project!

344

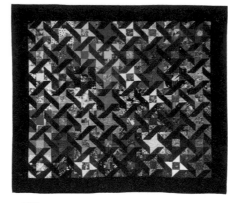

486

79

514

537

595

455

200

342

† 89 REFLECTIONS OF A SALINE LAND
95 CM X 110 CM (38 IN X 44 IN)
BY ALISON MUIR, NEUTRAL BAY, NEW SOUTH WALES
APPLIQUED, MACHINE PIECED AND QUILTED; SILK, ORGANZA

A passionate environmentalist, Alison is concerned about the continuing salination of Australia's waterways and the recent revelation that silt is closing the mouth of the mighty Murray River. Overuse and mismanagement of water has caused the water table to rise, bringing increased salt levels to surrounding farming areas. *Reflections of a Saline Land* is an expression of Alison's deep concern for the land and its preservation.

Using silks, some hand dyed, Alison has 'glued' shapes in place using fusible webbing. Following a simple sketch of the image, Alison free cuts the pieces and lets the fabric tell the story. She cuts several squiggly lines and then cuts them in sections ready for placement. This is a technique she has been working with and developing for five years.

Alison's work is included in the Colours of Australia touring exhibition and the Australia Dreaming collection. In 1999, she was one of the artists in A Sense of Place, an exhibition of textile art in Canberra, ACT. Her quilts are included in many private collections in Australia.

345

285

360

185

366

481

601

364

351

102

209

223

240

† **105 AUSTRALIAN KOOKABURRA**
121 CM X 124 CM (48 IN X 49 IN)
BY LEE WHITE, HEIDELBERG, VICTORIA
HAND APPLIQUED AND HAND QUILTED; COTTON

Creating original Australiana designs is nothing new for Lee White, who designs and markets a unique range of patterns featuring Australian wildflowers and birds. Often, inspiration for a new design comes from photographs Lee has taken while travelling through one of Australia's many isolated bush areas. The design for *Australian Kookaburra* was inspired by such a photograph, taken in the Grampian Mountains of Victoria.

Lee uses traditional skills to execute her original designs, preferring to work by hand. Her quilt, *My Australia*, won the Sydney to Atlanta Quilt Contest and was sent to Atlanta for the 1996 Olympic Games as a gift from Australia. In 1999, Lee was awarded Best of Show in the Victorian Quilters' Exhibition.

581

113

370

373

541

116

543

115

302

589

395

† 570 PURSUING THE DREAM
99 CM X 108 CM (40 IN X 43 IN)
BY LARAINE PICKETT, CARRARA, QUEENSLAND
MACHINE PIECED AND QUILTED; COTTON, SOME HAND DYED

Pursuing the Dream is not about winning but overcoming the challenges and difficulties all athletes face just to make the team. With a track in Olympic colours central to the design, Laraine has included a wheel to represent Australia's Paralympians. Surrounding the centre is the blue ocean and the red outback of Australia. Stylised fireworks and sail boats herald celebration with the coming together of many nations during the Games.

Using her preferred methods, Laraine cut out many squares of fabric to enable her to tone and blend colours. She roughly mapped out her ideas on a large piece of paper and added colour to her design concept while it remained on the floor. Having made the track and put it in place, Laraine proceeded to 'fill in' the remaining areas with squares of fabric, some of which had been dyed for this project.

Laraine often creates special quilts in response to a challenge and she enjoys making quilts dealing with political or women's issues. A recent work, expressing her concern regarding over-development of the Gold Coast area in Queensland, It has been acquired by the Gold Coast City Council. Her work was exhibited as part of the Art in Textile exhibition in Queensland and included in The Australian Bounty exhibition travelling to France in 2000.

273

143

135

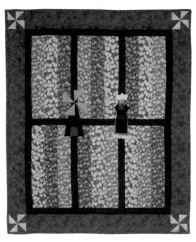

464

57

328

349

† 484

441

254 SOMEWHERE ALONG THE WAY
134 cm x 74 cm (53 in x 29 in)
By Lorraine Smith, Mudgee, New South Wales
MACHINE PIECED AND MACHINE QUILTED, HAND APPLIQUED AND EMBROIDERED; COTTON

Sue-Ellen Lovett is a well-known visually-impaired Paralympian who competed in equestrian events at the Atlanta Paralympic Games. Dedicated to raising community awareness of the Paralympic Games, Sue-Ellen undertakes long distance rides with her guide dog, Eccles, and her horse, Mudgee. Sue-Ellen's ride from Brisbane to Sydney was Lorraine's inspiration for her quilt, *Somewhere Along the Way*.

Imagining the Australian countryside through which Sue-Ellen would have passed, Lorraine developed five panels to depict the various stages of the journey, with Sydney Harbour as the final destination. To create the images, Lorraine used fusible web, appliqued with machine buttonhole stitching and 45 degree and straight strip piecing for the backgrounds. Some sections, such as the Sydney Harbour Bridge, were worked by hand.

Lorraine is a quilter with ten years experience. Most of her techniques are learned from avid reading and attendance at quilting workshops in Mudgee. Her work was featured in *A Quilter's Garden* by Caroline Price. In 1999, Lorraine was delighted to be awarded third place in a national block competition.

39

63

502

429

46

44

560

† 405 REFLECTIONS OF THE SYDNEY OPERA HOUSE
120 CM X 120 CM (48 IN X 48 IN)
BY CECILY DUNSTALL, MURRUMBATEMAN, NEW SOUTH WALES
MACHINE PIECED, MACHINE APPLIQUED AND MACHINE QUILTED; COTTON

To celebrate her love of Sydney's favourite icon, Cecily has created a textile masterpiece featuring a wonderful blend of traditional patchwork images and a stunning view of the Opera House. As a young woman in Sydney, Cecily remembers the controversy and excitement surrounding the construction of the Opera House. She still enjoys the occasional trip to the opera at her much-loved Opera House. *Reflections*, the theme of the 1999 Sydney Quilt Show, and the twenty-fifth anniversary of the Opera House opening in October 1998 were the inspirations for *Reflections of the Sydney Opera House.*

Central to the overall design is the Opera House, with the patchwork drawing the eye towards the machine appliqued trapunto sails. Cecily drew perspective lines onto freezer paper, then cut these out to form the templates for the patchwork. Machine quilting and stippling follow the perspective lines, while quilted gum leaves frame the picture. The quilt reflects on the many Australian artists who have performed in the House during the last twenty-five years—their names are written on the patchwork—while the appliqued music is the first line of the Australian national anthem.

Cecily has a passionate interest in artistic expression, having maintained a keen interest in art in education during her many years as a teacher. Quiltmaking has given her a new arena for this expression.

91

321

536

597

445

357

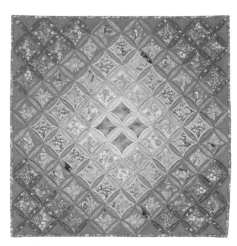

129

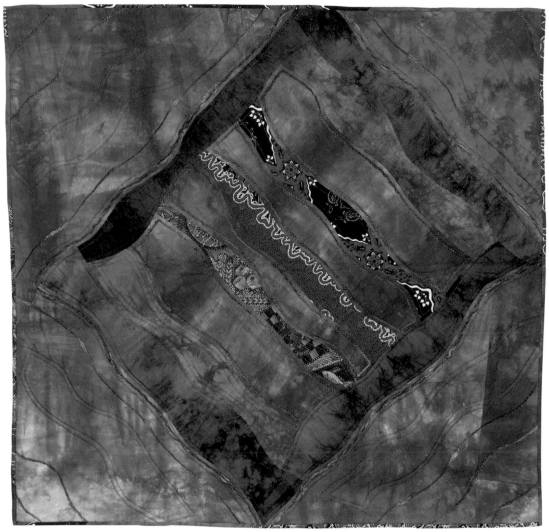

136 THE PINNACLE
100 CM X **97** CM **(40** IN X **38** IN**)**
BY YVONNE VOSS, WANGARATTA, VICTORIA
MACHINE PIECED AND MACHINE QUILTED; HAND DYED COTTON

An admirer of the achievement of athletes in general, Yvonne is particularly proud of the efforts of those selected for the Paralympic Games. She made *The Pinnacle* in recognition of the achievements of these athletes, with the hope that they will continue to succeed.

Using her own hand dyed fabrics, combined with Australian prints, Yvonne has created a contemporary landscape, which captures the excitement of the Games in an Australian context, coupled with a love of the rich earthy colours of the Australian outback.

Yvonne has been dabbling in quiltmaking since 1968, but has only been a passionate quiltmaker for the last fourteen years. For the past three years, she has been experimenting with printing and dyeing her own fabrics and finds this work very exciting. Having accepted several commissions to make traditional quilts, Yvonne now enjoys the freedom art quilts give her to explore her creativity.

227

339

5

419

522

426

296

157

224

428

334

53 CHALLENGES FROM THE TREE OF LIFE
101 CM X 101 CM (40 IN X 40 IN)
BY SUE WOOD, SOUTH CROYDON, VICTORIA
MACHINE PIECED AND QUILTED, CROSS-STITCH PANELS; COTTON

Sue comes from a family of avid sports enthusiasts. When the opportunity to participate in the QUILTS 2000 project arose, she decided to use her extensive collection of sporting images in her cross-stitch magazines, sourcing images for every Paralympic sport. The traditional Tree of Life block central to the design of the quilt seemed an appropriate choice when contemplating the lifestyle of the Paralympians.

With six sports not covered, Sue designed the remaining cross-stitch patterns herself. Using drawings of these six sports, she traced the images onto graph paper for her embroidery. Each cross stitch image was worked onto a 10 cm (4 in) square. Once the centre block was machine pieced, the cross-stitch images could be attached. Sue's love of traditional images is evident as she completed the quilt with a foundation pieced border of waratahs.

Sue is a self taught quilter who enjoys working by hand. Because of her commitments to the family business, she is not an active member of any group and enjoys working alone.

281

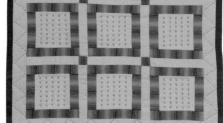

206

51

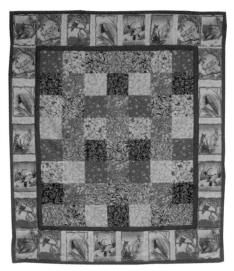

381

192

313

176

† **505 BANKSIA BUSH**
106 CM X **104** CM (**42** IN X **41** IN)
BY SUSAN MATHEWS, YARRAWONGO, VICTORIA
MACHINE PIECED AND MACHINE QUILTED; HAND DYED COTTON

Participation in a drawing class rekindled Susan's interest in Australian flora and led her to design the banksia block.

Banksia Bush, like most of her recent work, has evolved from explorations of many traditional forms of patchwork to the abandonment of the formal grid structure. Hand dyed fabrics create the basis of the work, providing a canvas for heavy machine quilting in an assortment of threads which emphasise the added design elements from the printed banksias.

Susan has formal qualifications as a secondary school art and craft teacher and she is a self-taught quiltmaker. She teaches extensively in Victoria and has undertaken several commissions. Susan's work has been exhibited locally, interstate and overseas. Until its untimely closure in 1999, Susan was a member of a cooperative, Quilt Gallery. Her work has been selected for the Australian Bounty Exhibition which tours France in 2000.

600

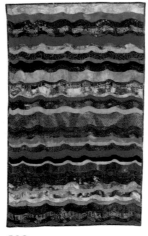

608

10

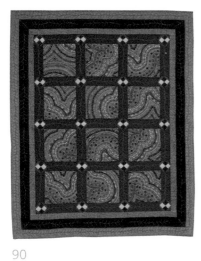

90

398

450

106

454

58

† **272 SPIRIT OF KATA TJUTA**
117 CM X 95 CM (46 IN X 38 IN)
BY GLORIA LOUGHMAN, KERANG, VICTORIA
HAND AND MACHINE APPLIQUED, MACHINE QUILTED AND EMBROIDERED; HAND DYED AND PAINTED COTTON

The Mount Olga Range perches on the edge of the Great Western Desert. Formed by rounded boulders embedded in fine sandstone, it has existed for over 200 million years. On a visit to the area, Gloria was captivated by its different moods as the rock surfaces change colour hour by hour. Her impressions of the area led to *Spirit of Kata Tjuta*, named for the mountain of many heads. A special-education teacher, Gloria has always been overwhelmed by her students strong spirit and will to succeed—much like the rebirth of the barren desert surrounding Kata Tjuta after a shower of rain. *Spirit of Kata Tjuta* is a fitting tribute to all those special people who overcome adversity, soaring to impossible heights.

For this quilt, Gloria first produced a full-sized drawing, then began to build up the foreground with specially prepared hand dyed and painted fabrics, layering them and using invisible applique to join them to the body of the quilt. The sky fabric was hand painted, as were some of the textures of the rocks. Machine embroidery was also used to add vegetation and texture on the rock surfaces.

Gloria has won major awards for her landscape quilts in Australia and Japan, and her work is greatly admired at exhibitions around the world. She is a teacher at the Yokohama International Quilt Exhibition in 2000 and at the New Zealand Symposium in 2001.

56

66

487

491

315

485

256

262

324

479 EVERGREEN
152 cm x 121 cm (61 in x 48 in)
By Julie Woods, North Epping, New South Wales
MACHINE PIECED, MACHINE APPLIQUED AND MACHINE QUILTED; COTTON

World Forest 2000 commissioned QUILTS 2000 to make a quilt which would represent their company and their mission to plant two million trees by the year 2000. The quilt was to include their logo and have an obvious 'trees and environment' theme. QUILTS 2000 approached Julie Woods, a Sydney textile artist well-known for her ability to approach new challenges with energy and expertise. *Evergreen* is the result.

Julie used the World Forest 2000 tree logo to create an avenue of trees stretching along the road, representing the planting of two million trees. The large logo of World Forest 2000 is the focal point of the quilt. She cut each piece of the background individually, then sewed it onto the backing fabric with invisible thread. The trees were backed with fusible webbing and after outlining the shapes on the wrong side, Julie satin-stitched the outline. Finally, she cut away the excess fabric.

Julie is a qualified fashion teacher with TAFE, and is an accredited teacher with the Quilters' Guild of New South Wales. Always interested in trying new techniques, Julie participates in many competitions and has won numerous awards, including first place and viewers' choice in the 1996 Lucindale Field Days Challenge in South Australia, and a first and second place in a national block competition. Her quilts have been exhibited internationally, including the Australia Dreaming exhibition in Nagoya, Japan, in 1995; in Houston at the Quilt Festival in 1997, and in Canada at the Biennial Exhibition in 1998.

162

584

85

244

180

24

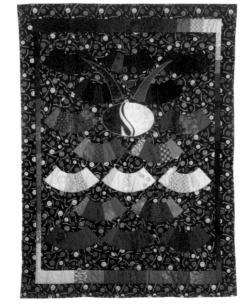

605

471

225

† 117 REJOICE IN AUSTRALIA
125 CM X 124 CM (50 IN X 49 IN)
BY PENELOPE NEIL, NAMBUCCA HEADS, NEW SOUTH WALES
HAND APPLIQUED, MACHINE QUILTED, EMBROIDERED; COTTON

In *Rejoice in Australia*, Penelope combines her love of the extraordinary beauty and diversity of Australia, her adopted country, with her interpretation of what the Paralympic Games mean to Australia, as the world comes together for the 2000 Games. Her quilt reflects not only the beauty of the country, but the importance of sharing with others, in peaceful interaction through sport.

Rejoice in Australia is Penelope's third applique work. The techniques were explored through trial-and-error, as Penelope began with a rough, full-size sketch then cut the fabric—sometimes with no pattern. To get just the right effect, she often reapplied the individual images several times.

Penelope embraced quilting in 1998. The first block she made won second place in a national competition. Her first quilt won first place in the Verandah Post Patchworkers Challenge and her second quilt won second place in The Toowoomba Challenge. Totally self-taught, Penelope enjoys experimentation and working with her original designs.

500

191

61

439

319

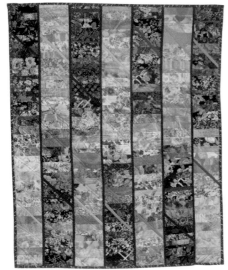

411

529

219

286 GO, AUSTRALIA, GO!
86 CM X 134 CM (34 IN X 53 IN)
BY BETH ROBERTS, LOWER MITCHAM, SOUTH AUSTRALIA
MACHINE PIECED, MACHINE QUILTED AND MACHINE EMBROIDERED; HAND PAINTED AND HAND DYED; COTTON

The attributes of Paralympic athletes embody the spirit of Australia as they strive for perfection with perseverance and overcome almost insurmountable odds. Their determination and purpose parallels the spirit shown by generations of Australians to overcome the devastation of fires, floods and droughts. Greek athletes signify the history of the Olympic Games, while floral emblems from each state and the golden wattle, Australia's national floral emblem, show that all Australia is involved in supporting the Sydney 2000 Paralympic Games. Lizzie, the mascot, leads the athletes to victory as the crowd roars 'Go Australia Go!'. Beth Roberts has encapsulated these thoughts in her quilt *Go, Australia, Go!*

Some images on the quilt are drawn with the machine needle and thread, while others are appliqued using a buttonhole stitch. For the wattle, Beth used a real spray of wattle, and traced around the leaves onto organza. She then satin stitched over fishing line to achieve the desired result.

For Beth, traditional quilt patterns are only a base for her innovative designs incorporating extensive machine embroidery. Her work has been exhibited in national exhibitions including The Festival of Wool at the National Textile Museum in 1997. Beth held a retrospective exhibition during the National Embroiderers' Conference in Adelaide in 1999. She has received many awards, including first prize in the Pictorial Miniature section of the South Australian Quilters' Guild exhibition in 1998, and an honourable mention at the Dame Mary Durack Outback Crafts Awards in 1999.

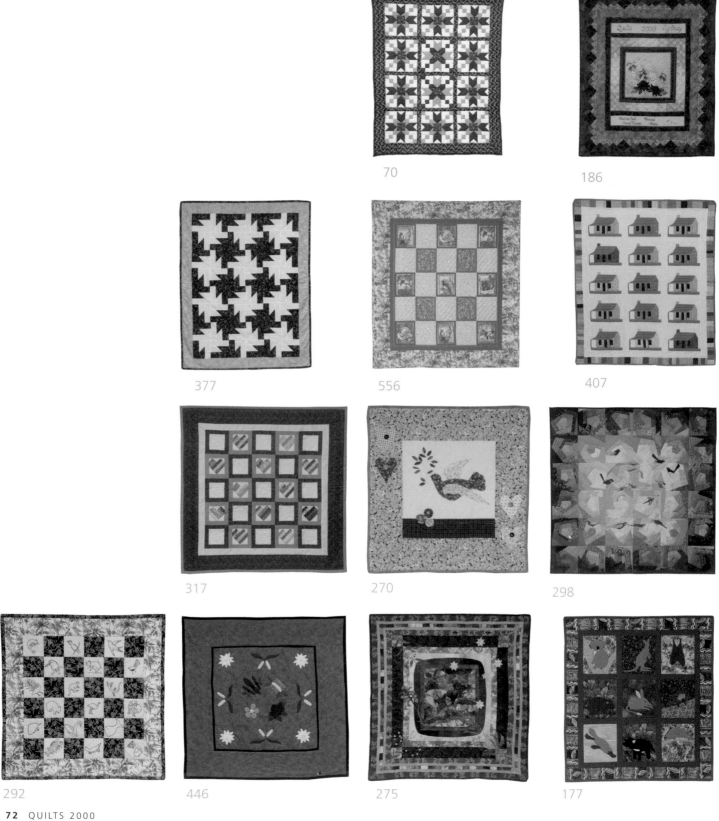

70

186

377

556

407

317

270

298

292

446

275

177

† 81 SPRING IN THE SUNBURNT COUNTRY
111 CM X 127 CM (44 IN X 50 IN)
BY JENNY BOWKER, GARRAN, AUSTRALIAN CAPITAL TERRITORY
MACHINE APPLIQUED AND MACHINE QUILTED; COTTON FABRIC, WOOL BATTING

Spring in the Sunburnt Country captures both the majestic feeling of the big granite tors and the spill of colour from wildflowers during an Australian Spring. Inspired by a photograph of the Tidbinbilla area in the Australian Capital Territory, Jenny used traditional blocks to express her love of the countryside. While each block is unique and separate, joined together they form a cohesive whole, making an interesting picture. The star block represents Australia's Paralympic stars, who start with a major obstacle and have to overcome it to pursue their sport.

Jenny uses a simple technique of translating a photographic image into a series of templates. Fabric is adhered to a background and held in place with soft-edge machine applique to achieve the blurred edges of the landscape. These sections are combined with traditional blocks, made with carefully selected fabrics, to complete the picture.

A prolific quiltmaker since completing a Bachelor of Arts (Visual) in 1997, Jenny has received several major awards, including first prize in the Amateur Innovative section of the Sydney Quilt Show, 1999, and 'Best of Show' in Quilt-O-Rama, Queensland, in 1999. She is a much sought-after tutor, specialising in using traditional blocks to interpret a landscape.

242

568

498

304

368

492

314

482

320

472 AND THEY WILL RISE UP WITH WINGS AS EAGLES
80 CM X 100 CM (32 IN X 40 IN)
BY MARGARET WALLACE, KALARU, NEW SOUTH WALES
HAND AND MACHINE PIECED, HAND AND FREE MACHINE EMBROIDERY, MACHINE QUILTING; COTTON, SOME HAND DYED AND PAINTED

When contemplating the power and performance of the Paralympians, Margaret's thoughts turned to the verse from the Bible in Isiah 40:31, 'They shall rise up with wings like eagles'. She had often admired the majestic sea eagles around Blackfellows Lake in her home town of Kalaru on the south coast of New South Wales and decided to use this image in her quilt *And They Will Rise Up With Wings As Eagles* as a tribute to the Paralympians.

Incorporating her love of painting, piecing and free machine embroidery, Margaret has designed her quilt to include wildflowers prevalent in her local area. Before painting the background, she applied a resist to block out the shapes of the yellow Hibbertia scandens and the flannel flowers. Dyed and hand painted fabrics were used to get just the right gradation of colour for the border of blocks. The sea eagle is the star, its position emphasised by the machine quilting lines in the lake.

Margaret began quilting in 1993 when she joined the Bega Quilters. She now combines her love of painting with the joy of working with textiles. To interpret her ideas, she was forced to learn to sew and now feels quite at home painting with a brush or her sewing machine. Her entry in the Australian Quilts for Kids competition in 1999 won first place in the Canberra section.

305

11

271

511

449

425

† 474

260

33

166

261

† 38 PARTY PARTY 2000

123 cm x **145** cm (**49** in x **58** in)
BY CAROLYN SWART, TURRAMURRA, NEW SOUTH WALES
MACHINE PIECED CRAZY PATCHWORK, MACHINE APPLIQUE; COTTON AND SYNTHETICS, SOME OVERDYED

In *Party Party 2000*, Carolyn captures the spirit of celebration, of people coming together from all over the world to Sydney to compete in and enjoy the Paralympic Games. Each athlete is a star in his own right, and everyone who visits this beautiful sun-drenched country will find many reasons to party.

Many different fabrics were used in the crazy patch background, including cotton, silk and hand painted fabric. The quilt is totally machine made from an original design and won second prize in the Innovative section of the Sydney Quilt Exhibition in 1999.

Carolyn is a self-taught quiltmaker and fibre artist, who has been designing and making quilts since 1989. She shows a strong understanding of colour and texture, evident in her dazzling wallhangings. Carolyn's work has been exhibited all over Australia and in Japan, the United States and Europe. She was the feature artist on a national television programme and is a regular contributor to national quilting magazines. Currently, she is working on an exhibition of quilts for a private gallery in Europe.

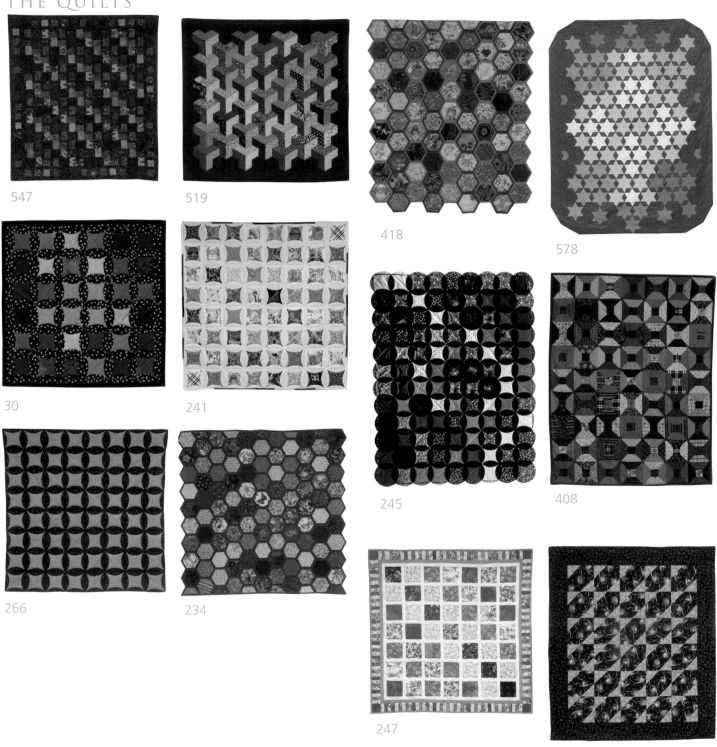

547

519

418

578

30

241

266

234

245

408

247

607

† **235 UNDER AUSSIE SKIES**
129 cm x 101 cm (51 in x 40 in)
By Adina Sullivan, South Grafton, New South Wales
Hand pieced, machine quilted; cotton

All along the eastern coast of Australia, on perfect summer days, the sky becomes the most beautiful blue and shimmers in the heat of the sun. In *Under Aussie Skies*, Adina captures the delight of the summer sky, incorporating the Mariner's Compass stars for which she is renowned.

Adina drafted the twelve-pointed Mariner's Compass to fit into a six-sided hexagon onto freezer paper. She then pieced the compasses by hand over the cut-out freezer paper, using the English piecing method. The quilt is machine quilted by free motion with an overall feather design.

Adina began quiltmaking ten years ago in Mt Isa, an outback mining town in western Queensland. She developed her own methods of drafting and piecing the Mariner's Compass in 1994 and since then has incorporated them in many of her quilts. While enjoying the accuracy of hand piecing, Adina prefers to machine quilt. Her work received international recognition when she won the Machine Quilting Award for a Wall Quilt at the American Quilters' Society exhibition in Paduca in 1997. She has also held solo exhibitions, in Grafton in 1998 and Tamworth in 1999, and is a popular tutor and speaker at conferences nationally.

284

580

598

88

† **422 YOU BEAUTY BENNETI**
92 CM X 134 CM (36 IN X 53 IN)
BY LORRAINE LAMOTHE, LAKE EACHAM, QUEENSLAND
PAINTED WHOLECLOTH, HEAVILY HAND QUILTED; COTTON

Lorraine believes that insects are a metaphor for the futility of preconceived notions and arbitrary decisions about art and the 'form vs. function' argument. Many in the art world do not perceive textile works as art—just as many people feel that insects are far from beautiful. Contrary to this view, Lorraine delights in insects, and believes the weevil to be the most beautiful item in her extensive insect collection. She uses the weevil as the inspiration for *You Beauty Benneti*, capturing the dimpling on the back of a weevil with the heavy quilting.

'If you hate the insect because of preconceived notions, but like the art work, maybe you have misjudged the insect,' Lorraine postulates. She believes that the Paralympians fight the same prejudice.

109

67

212

294

118

393

204

† 122 **COLOURSCAPE**
91 cm x **118** cm **(36** in x **47** in)
BY SUZIE CHEEL, ROZELLE, NEW SOUTH WALES
MACHINE PIECED, HAND QUILTED; HAND PAINTED WOOL, SILK

The colours, shapes and patterns of Australia, as seen in the ever-changing landscape, people and culture, were the inspiration for Suzie's first quilt, *Colourscape*. Since many quilters had been using her hand painted silk and wool off-cuts for their quilts, making her own quilt was a natural progression.

With encouragement and a little coaching from her friend Dianne Finnegan, Suzie constructed the top of the quilt, using a variety of hand painted wool crepe fabrics and off-cuts from wool jackets she had produced over the last ten years. The quilt is backed by a piece of hand painted silk which was originally destined to become a shirt. Suzie found that in making *Colourscape*, she has discovered a new vehicle for self-expression with the stitching a rewarding, relaxing, meditative process. Suzie readily donated her first art quilt to QUILTS 2000 in recognition of those who rise above their personal challenges and show us that there is hope for all of us.

Suzie Cheel is a professional textile artist. Through her business, Suzie Cheel Handpainted Originals, she has exhibited and sold her hand painted textiles in Australia and the United States since 1986. Special milestones for Suzie were being awarded the Alice Annual Craft Prize, in Alice Springs in 1980 and 1997; being selected for the Tamworth Fibre Exhibition in 1990, and receiving the Award of Excellence for hand painted silk from the Australian Silk Corporation at the Australian Craft Show, 1991. She has been a regular contributor to *Australian Textile Fibre Forum* since 1991, writing on 'Making a Living in Textile Art'.

154

263

210

205

258

251

259

257

307

156 MILLENNIUM BUG
100 CM X 150 CM (40 IN X 60 IN)
BY DIJANNE CEVAAL, GELLIBRAND, VICTORIA
MACHINE PIECED, MACHINE APPLIQUED AND MACHINE QUILTED; HAND DYED COTTON, FEATHERS

The *Millennium Bug* takes a tongue-in-cheek look at the fuss surrounding Y2K compliance for old computers and the 'millenium bug'. At the same time, Dijanne takes a deeper look at how the world is consuming its natural resources, with the computer as the ultimate symbol of consumption. The quilt was awarded Best of Show in the South Australian Quilters' Guild exhibition Towards the New Millennium, in 1998.

Dijanne dyed fabrics and used freehand applique to create the visual image. The work is embellished with some feathers and heavy machine stitching.

Dijanne Cevaal is a professional quiltmaker, with numerous national and international awards to her credit. Her work received an Honorable Mention in the Pacific International Quilt Festival in 1997 and a judge's ribbon from Penny Nii. Dijanne is the only Australian included in the Expressions of Freedom Exhibition, organised by the James Foundation and the University of Nebraska in the United States, where participants were invited to interpret an article of the United Nations Charter. Her prize-wining quilt in the 1997 Chassy D'Or was acquired by the Chateau de Chassy Museum, and in 2000, Dijanne participates in a studio residency at Chateau Chassy en Morvan, taking with her the Australian Bounty Exhibition of quilts.

+ 526

380

338

453

169

178

557 SUNSET OVER THE BRINDABELLAS
90 cm x 93 cm (36 in x 37 in)
By Margaret Wright, Killara, new south wales
Machine pieced and quilted; hand dyed cotton

Sunrise and sunset are reflective times of day for Margaret. However, living in the city, the ever changing expanse of sky which give her much joy, is so often limited to just a fraction of the grand scale of that above the vast expanses of the Australian countryside. So Margaret is a regular visitor to the Australian Capitol Territory, where wonderful sunsets can be enjoyed, framed by the surrounding mountain range, The Brindabellas. Margaret was able to capture one of these stunning and powerful sunsets on film which inspired her to make *Sunset over the Brindabellas.*

Using Jane Gibson's hand dyed fabrics, Margaret took the traditional block, Square in a Square, and graduated colour to interpret the sunset landscape. The quilt is dedicated to Australia's Paralympians who collectively inspired the QUILTS 2000 project.

Margaret is chairman of the QUILTS 2000 committee and the instigator of the project. She is a freelance journalist, writing articles on all aspects of quilting with a particular interest in Japanese textiles. Her popularity as an outstanding lecturer continues to grow and she receives many invitations to lecture on a broad range of quilt related topics. She is a founding member of the Australian Quilt Study Group.

423

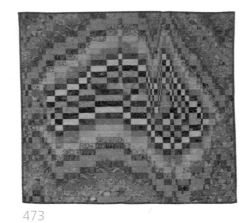

473

52

406

499

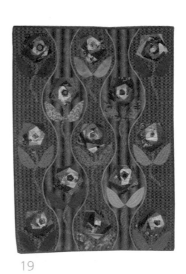

19

73

78

194

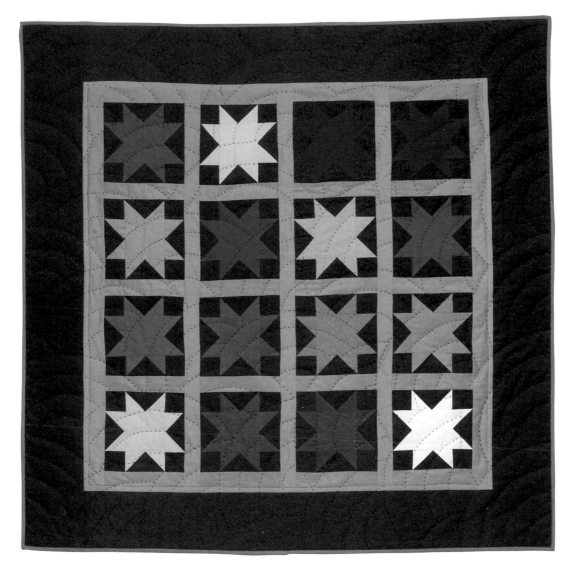

593 GOOD OLD FASHIONED STARS
131 cm x 131 cm (52 in x 52 in)
By Karen Fail, hornsby heights, new south wales
Machine pieced, hand quilted; cotton

Fascinated by the light and magic in Amish quilts seen in *Lit from Within,* an exhibition of Amish quilts from the Esprit collection, Karen has made several Amish style quilts, experimenting with the juxtaposition of brilliant colours and dull, sombre hues. Her goal is to position the colours so that the quilt appears 'lit from within'.

A collection of Sawtooth Stars, made using modern cutting and machine piecing methods, was the basis for the quilt. Made as an experiment in colour, it feature a range of red and pink stars set against a dull brown background. The small brilliant aqua border adds the surprise, so common in traditional Amish quilts. The quilting pattern was marked using different sized plates—the original templates.

Karen is an internationally known author, lecturer and teacher. Her books reflect her passion for quiltmakers and the stories behind their quilts. She has initiated many highly successful events, including *Colours of Australia*, *The Sydney Quilt Festival* and *QuiltSkills*. As an editor for J. B. Fairfax Press (Australia), she encouraged many Australian quilters to become authors and promoted them internationally. She is particularly interested in friendship quilts and one of her books, *Between Friends*, details the history of Australian friendship quilts.

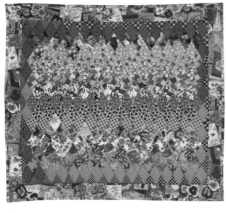

3

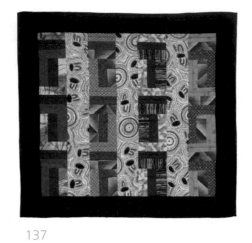

137

331

215

92

170

434

82

516

† 138 DO YOUR BEST NO MATTER WHAT
112 CM X 98 CM (45 IN X 39 IN)
BY LEANNE McGILL, KATHERINE, NORTHERN TERRITORY
MACHINE PIECED, HAND APPLIQUED, MACHINE QUILTED; HAND PRINTED TIWI FABRICS, COTTON

The McGill family travels extensively in their nine-tonne, twin-cab truck. In 1999, they notched up 24,000 km (15,000 miles) around Australia and New Zealand. For the trip, Leanne carefully stores her sewing supplies, her husband's work tools and the children's books, toys and schoolwork under the truck canopy. Her precious sewing machine sits in a sturdy box, purpose-built to withstand the rough roads of Australia's outback.

Do Your Best No Matter What, named after the family's motto, was made on a friend's rural property on the banks of the Katherine River, during the beautiful weather of the dry season of 1999. Leanne set up a table, chair and her sewing machine under a large tree, on a very large piece of strong plastic as the floor. As is often the case, she ended up sitting on the ground cutting and arranging her collection of hand printed Tiwi fabrics. The fabrics she chose for the quilt reflect the Top End of the Northern Territory, with its rocky cliffs, white and purple skies, and grey-blue rivers. Using quarter-square triangles as the basic unit, Leanne arranged the blocks to loosely resemble the local landscape shapes, appliqueing the lines on by hand.

For the people of Katherine, the agricultural shows in Darwin, Fred's Pass and Katherine are opportunities to exhibit a great range of items from stud cattle to fine needlework. Leanne's quilts have won several awards, including Best Large Quilt at The Royal Darwin Agricultural Show. Leanne has given many of her quilts away or donated them to charity. She delights in passing on the joy of creating something beautiful with textiles to her two boys.

† 561

49

72

55

358

410

495

203

507

131 CHILDHOOD DREAMING
115 CM X 85 CM (46 IN X 34 IN)
JENNY SEARLE, HORNSBY HEIGHTS, NEW SOUTH WALES
MACHINE PIECED, HAND APPLIQUED, HAND QUILTED; COTTON, SOME BLEACHED AND STENCILLED, NET

As a child, Jenny lived in Wahroongah, a Sydney suburb, when her house was the only one in the street. She and her brothers played in the nearby bush and their games often centred around a large rock. They created all sorts of stories about the Aboriginal people who carved the images into the rock and dreamed about the children who would have played around it. The street is now part of suburbia, and the rock is carefully preserved and unnoticed, covered by a verandah. Jenny has encapsulated her memories of those happy times in *Childhood Dreaming*.

Several techniques have been used to emulate the images of the rock and surrounds. Remembering that Aboriginal people used to spatter ochre paint from their mouths to form images on rock faces, Jenny used bleach to spatter onto brown and black fabric, creating hands and other images using cut-outs of Australian animals. Eucalyptus leaves were cut from fabric and applied roughly across the quilt, just like the leaves falling on the rock. Large white stitches represent the carvings on the rock. Jenny has made clever use of fabric designed by Jimmy Pyke, an indigenous Australian, to represent traditional dot paintings. The entire quilt has been put together as a collage using net overlay and raw-edged applique.

Jenny has been quilting for ten years and enjoys creating original designs using new techniques. She won first prize in the Eastwood Black and White Challenge in 1992. The winning quilt was acquired for a private collection in the United States of America.

THE QUILTS

490

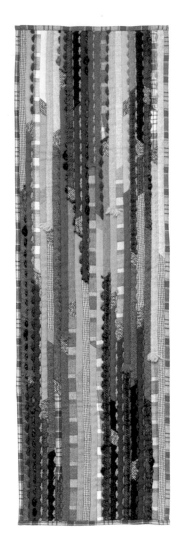

528

535

571

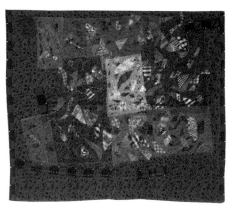

497

21

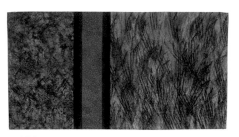

461

112

94 QUILTS 2000

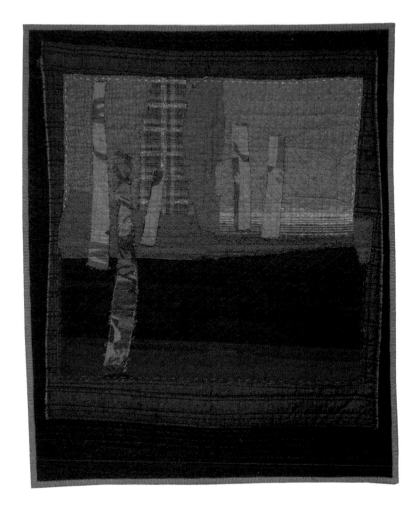

558 AFTERMATH
88 cm x 107 cm (35 in x 42 in)
By Judy Hooworth, Terrey Hills, New South Wales
Hand and machine appliqued, hand and machine stitched, machine quilted; found screen print and wool scraps, cotton and cotton blends

A desolate landscape emerged as Judy constructed a collage from fabric scraps, rescued from the cleaning rag cupboard at Kuringai Art Centre where she teaches. She used the fabrics as they were, with as little alteration to their found shape as possible. The result was *Aftermath*.

Judy has formal qualifications from the National Art School in Sydney and has taught quiltmaking since 1981, giving workshops throughout Australia and more recently in New Zealand, Germany and the United States As president of the Quilters' Guild in 1989, Judy initiated The New Quilt, an exhibition of art quilts at the Manly Art Gallery and Museum and coordinated this annual event for the next eight years.

Her quilts have been shown in major exhibitions in Australia and overseas, including Visions in 1992 and Quilt National in 1993 and 1999 with many acquired for private and public collections. Judy coordinated Quilt Art Australia ... From the Bush to the Sea which was seen in Gröbenzell, German, and the Sydney Quilt Festival, 1999. The recipient of many prizes and awards, Judy received the 1994 Quilters' Guild scholarship and a professional development grant from the Australia Council in 1995. She co-authored the book *Spectacular Scraps* with Margaret Rolfe.

447

443

333

330

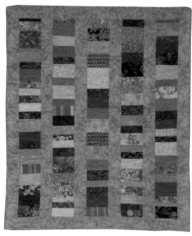

276

97

17

409

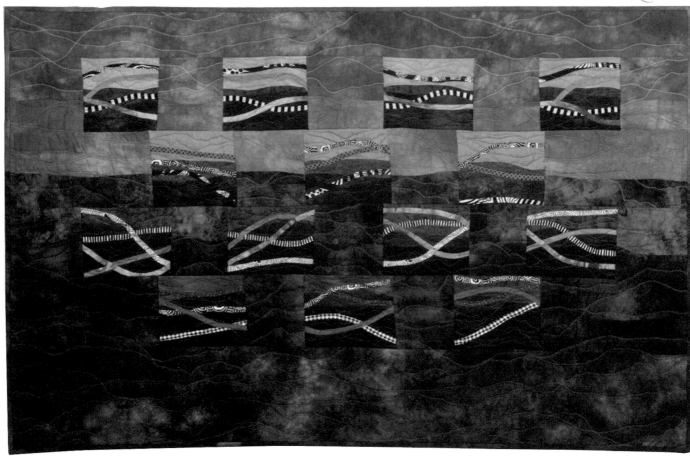

47 BUSHFIRE WEATHER
124 CM X **81** CM (**49** IN X **32** IN)
BY ALISON SCHWABE, SHELLEY, WESTERN AUSTRALIA
MACHINE PIECED AND MACHINE QUILTED; COTTON, SOME HAND DYED

The Australian landscape has been greatly influenced by the action of fire. The indigenous people of Australia saw the importance of the spirit of fire in the natural cycle of life, using its power to benefit Man, while maintaining a sense of awe and respect for it. With good reason, early European settlers feared sudden tragedy and devastation when fire is out of control and as a result, fire makes dramatic appearances in Australia's modern bush folklore and literature.

Bushfire Weather is typical of Alison's work where she employs pattern-free cutting, machine piecing and machine quilting.

Since 1976, stitchery has been Alison's medium of choice for personal expression. Her textile works have always been inspired by landscape patterns and textures. Since 1988, she has exhibited her quilted textiles in solo and group shows in Japan, German, Uruguay, the United Kingdom and the United States, the latter at Quilt National in 1993 and 1995. Her work has been seen in most Australian states, including solos shows for the Craft Council in Darwin and Hobart in 1999, and the New Quilt Exhibition at the Manly Gallery, New South Wales, from 1996-1999. Alison was artist in residence in Katherine in the Northern Territory from May to June 1998, and is an accredited quilt valuer and teacher with the West Australian Quilters' Association.

† 93

518

548

609

577

524

389

139

554

12 RIPPLES
146 CM X 88 CM (58 IN X 35 IN)
BY DIANNE FINNEGAN, LANE COVE, NEW SOUTH WALES
MACHINE PIECED AND MACHINE QUILTED; COTTON

The concentric circles of *Ripples* spread out from the centre, suggesting the interaction of people brought together by the games. They reflect the form of the Olympic rings and the networks and friendships formed through the community activities of QUILTS 2000. The quilt is open-sided suggesting continuity and the outward movement of these networks, without boundaries.

Pieces for *Ripples* have been cut freeform without the use of a ruler, creating irregular strips for this variation on the traditional log cabin. Dianne has incorporated green hand dyed fabrics for their natural textured effect and to encompass the green and gold Australian theme.

Author of *Piece by Piece—The Complete Book of Australian Quiltmaking* and *The Quilters Kaleidoscope*, as well as many articles, Dianne has developed an international reputation during her long involvement in the quilt world. She has taught in Australia, the United Kingdom and the United States, and was named International Quilting Teacher for 1995, winning a scholarship to the International Quilt Festival in Houston. She was also named one of the 88 leaders of the quilt world by Japanese publisher, Nihon Vogue.

458

562

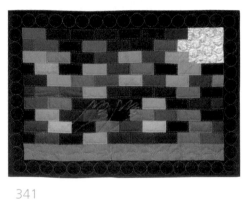

341

50

32

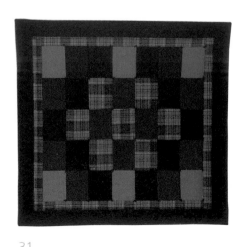

31

77

20

† **189 NATIONAL PRIDE** (LEFT), **190 NATURAL POWER**
98 CM X 134 CM (39 IN X 53 IN)
BY THE EPPING QUILTERS, EPPING, NEW SOUTH WALES
MACHINE PIECED, MACHINE AND HAND APPLIQUED, MACHINE EMBROIDERED; VARIETY OF FABRICS

National Pride features five achievements of Australia's pioneering days—the wool industry, opal mining, the Flying Doctor Service, The School of the Air and the mining industry. The blocks are set on a pieced background representing the movement and strength of the nation.

Natural Power represents five natural disasters that bond people together—fire, drought, floods, cyclones and hailstorms.

Frances Loder, a member of the Epping Quilters and a former fabric designer, originated the concept and designed the blocks. Each quilt features prominently the large stars which form the Southern Cross, a powerful emblem of Australia.

Epping Quilters meet weekly for 'Show and Tell' and regularly organise workshops for their members. Their talents range far beyond quiltmaking, with many fine embroiderers, knitters and crocheters in the group. Their biannual exhibition attracts visitors from all over Sydney and surrounding areas.

323

359

325

222

306

308

16

150

297

† 26 BLAZE
100 CM X 101 CM (40 IN X 40 IN)
BY DIANNE FIRTH, TURNER, AUSTRALIAN CAPITAL TERRITORY
MACHINE PIECED AND MACHINE QUILTED; COTTON

Blaze captures the glowing embers of a fire, the hot sun and the 'blaze of glory' for all winning athletes. Inspired by the Paralympians' desire for success, Dianne has reduced the idea to a minimum of line, form, colour and texture to create this quilt.

Using her ordered piecing technique, she has blended colour and tone to achieve a luminous quality.

Since 1982, Dianne has been producing art quilts for exhibition and sale. She has received numerous awards and her work has been selected for national and international exhibitions. Diane is represented in public and private collections in Australia, Europe and the United States. Her work has been selected for two major European exhibitions in 2000.

278

237

103

29

23

132

282

133

385

† **239 ECHIDNA**
90 CM X 90 CM (36 IN X 36 IN)
BY FRANCES MULHOLLAND, TOOWOOMBA, QUEENSLAND
MACHINE APPLIQUED AND MACHINE QUILTED; COTTON AND HAND DYED FURNISHING FABRIC

On a drive along a dusty, lonely country road, Frances had to stop the car to allow a mother echidna and her baby to cross. Here was a real success story of survival against adversity—a powerful car stopped in its tracks by this tiny creature. More than that, it was vulnerability triumphing against all odds, with quiet determination and strength. Because of this experience, Frances chose the echidna to represent the bravery of spirit in people with a disability.

Beginning with a small crayon drawing of an echidna, Frances developed *Echidna*. 'Painting' with scraps of fabric, she adhered the features and border to the background, adding extensive machine embroidery to the image. Once layered, the quilt was heavily machine quilted.

Despite her busy life as a doctor, Frances is constantly investigating new techniques, including the effects of 'painting' pictures with scraps of fabric, embellished with extensive machine embroidery and quilting. Her aim is to capture a memory or portray a human emotion in the medium she is most comfortable with—fabric and thread.

476

587

576

376

187

417

563

221

378

582

161

630

1 WINDOW ON MURCHISON
138 CM X 102 CM (55 IN X 41 IN)
BY CYNTHIA MORGAN, CALOUNDRA, QUEENSLAND
MACHINE STITCHED AND MACHINE QUILTED; HAND DYED COTTON

Window on Murchison was inspired by a trip to the Murchison River area in Western Australia. On the top of a rocky escarpment, there is an extraordinary jagged hole through which two different views of the river can be seen on either side of the huge column of rock. It is this spectacle that Cynthia represents in her quilt.

The quilt was designed directly onto the quilt sandwich. Working with hand dyed fabrics, Cynthia worked intuitively with the fabrics, from the top down, overlapping the cut or torn raw edges, then machine stitched them together. She then further embellished the central 'view' with hand stitching and embroidery.

Cynthia is one of Australia's favourite quilt artists, whose work has been exhibited nationally and internationally. Exhibitions featuring her work include Threads of Journey, which visited twenty-two countries, Australia Dreaming in Japan and A Celebration of Nature in the United States. As a result of these exhibitions, Cynthia has received corporate and private commissions for art quilt wallhangings in her Barrier Reef, Rainforest and Australian Outback series, from both Australia and overseas. She is an experienced tutor and has published a book on her work, *A Quilter's Journey—Inspiration to Culmination*.

THE QUILTS

60

171

299

397

199

585

83

559

355

110

164

573

† **440 HOT NORTH WIND**
145 CM X 145 CM (58 IN X 58 IN)
BY BARBARA MACEY, MOUNT WAVERLEY, VICTORIA
MACHINE SEWN, MACHINE EMBELLISHED; COTTON

During summer, south-eastern Australia is often seared by a hot wind from the north. It drives the last of the moisture from the once-lush grass. Trees drop dry leaves and ribbons of bark. Smoke hides the sun. Animals flee. There is fear and confusion. A tiny spark is driven by heat and wind to devour the ready fuel. In an instant, it is a greedy killer, stunning the senses with heat, light and sound. In *Hot North Wind*, Barbara revives the memories of being trapped with her family by a wall of fire, close enough to singe their hair.

Hot North Wind is made in a contemporary crazy technique, an adaptation of a traditional method where the pieces are sewn directly onto a foundation fabric. After experimenting with the Log Cabin technique for a number of years, Barbara began exploring this related technique in 1985. The method requires no quilting.

Barbara has developed a distinctive style for her quilts, using foundation piecing with several of her quilts being acquired for public collections. She has had seven solo exhibitions, and her work has been represented in many group exhibitions, including The New Quilt exhibitions at the Manly Gallery. She was the first Australian to be selected for the prestigious Quilt National and subsequent touring exhibitions. Barbara is President of Ozquilt Network Inc., a nationwide organisation for contemporary quilters.

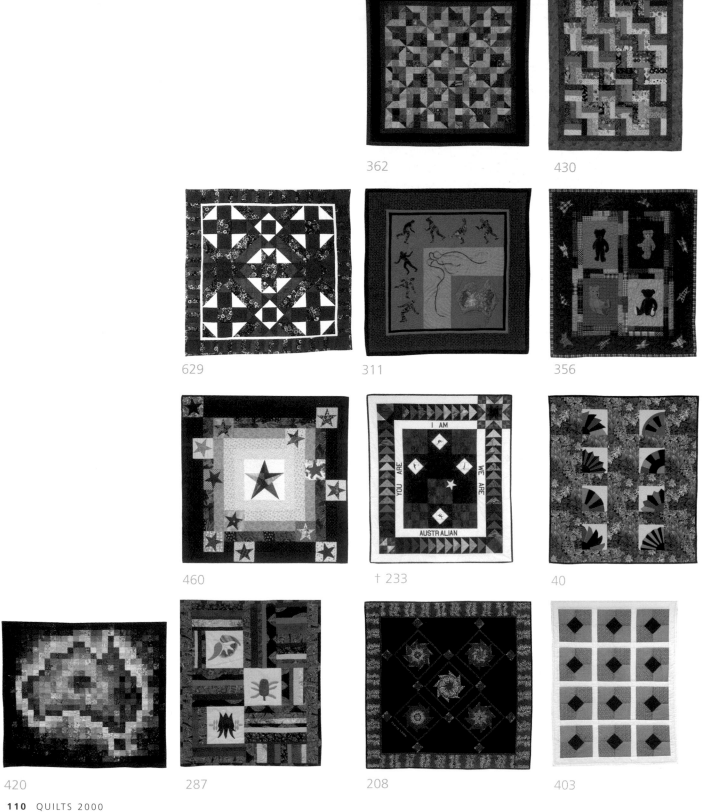

362

430

629

311

356

460

† 233

40

420

287

208

403

34 FLAMING STARS
112 CM X 112CM (45 IN X 45 IN)
BY JANE GIBSON, EPPING, NEW SOUTH WALES
MACHINE PIECED AND MACHINE QUILTED: COTTON

Flaming Stars is an award-winning quilt. It was originally made for a national competition in which it was awarded first place. Jane donated the quilt to QUILTS 2000 and it was selected to become the image on the first QUILTS 2000 pin.

Jane is adept at making complex traditional patterns look easy. The Feathered Star in *Flaming Stars* is pieced to perfection using a system of partial seams. Not one of the difficult corners needs to be set in, creating perfect Feathered Stars as the centrepiece of the quilt. To achieve the outstanding quilting, Jane marked the main elements onto tissue paper and positioned them onto the quilt, removing the tissue paper when the quilting was complete. She quilted the remaining elements using free machine quilting.

Jane is a member of the QUILTS 2000 committee, having previously been a committee member of The Quilters' Guild of NSW for three years. A regular winner at the Sydney Royal Easter Show, Jane's work has been published in *The Template, Down Under Quilts, Australia Dreaming,* and *Quilts Japan, 1997.* She has exhibited nationally, in Japan and in the United States.

165

13

124

152

101

181

387

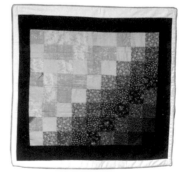

546

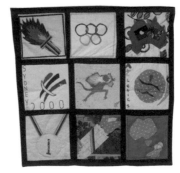

533

374

119

372

† 322 NAMBUCCA, OUR MOUNTAINS TO THE SEA
123 cm x **109** cm (**49** in x **43** in)
By The Art Collective, Nambucca Valley Phoenix Ltd, Bowraville, New South Wales
Hand painted blocks, machine pieced and machine quilted; cotton, heat-set paints

Members of the Art Collective have captured images from their lives for their quilt, *Nambucca, Our Mountains to the Sea*. These adults with special abilities and intellectual disabilities have chosen to make a living by selling their art. They have worked for the past five years to develop their skills and produce pieces for a local art gallery and café, sponsored by Nambucca Valley Phoenix Ltd. Their work includes painting on canvas, pottery, papier maché and sculpture.

This is their first quilt. Each artist chose a view of life in the Nambucca Valley to paint onto canvas. The rural and beach scenes were then sewn together, making a patchwork of the images to resemble a window. The quilt is very simply machine quilted.

The group had wanted to make a contribution to the Sydney 2000 Paralympic Games for some time and had approached SOCOG to find out how they could participate. There seemed no easy way for them to be involved, until they found out about QUILTS 2000—a project they very happily embraced.

290

483

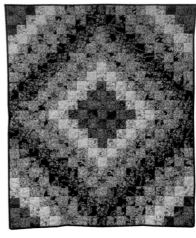

318

27

54

174

125

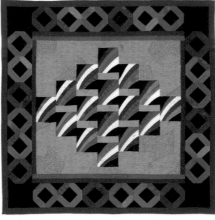

† 264

218

75 BLUE CLAM
100 CM X 100 CM (40 IN X 40 IN)
BY DENISE VANDERLUGT, PROSERPINE, QUEENSLAND
HAND APPLIQUED, HAND QUILTED AND HAND EMBROIDERED; COTTON

Blue Clam represents the special times Denise has had snorkelling over the Great Barrier Reef. The feeling is similar to walking in a garden, she says, with all its complexity of pattern and texture, shape and colour, endlessly changing as the light passes across the surface. The clam in its environment is not dissimilar to a person with a physical disability—restricted in its movement by being embedded in the reef, but no less important, no less beautiful than the colourful fish that move freely in and around the coral garden.

In making *Blue Clam*, Denise used her own method of constructed images, combining hand stitched applique and hand quilting with added embroidery, Suffolk puffs and reverse applique

Denise has been quiltmaking since 1982, and her hand stitched wallhangings are held in corporate, public and private collections in Australia and overseas. Her work represented Australia in the Memories of Childhood exhibition at the Museum of American Folk Art in 1988, and her entry in Quilts Covering Australia, a national touring exhibition in 1988 was later featured on a UNICEF card. Denise was featured in *Australian Artist* in 1990. Her work has been published widely in national and international magazines.

391

512

64

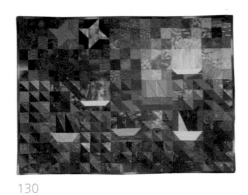

130

68

603

513

† 503 REACHING TOWARDS SYDNEY 2000
121 CM X **142** CM (**48** IN X **57** IN)
BY EVELYN PEPPER, WILLIAMSTOWN, VICTORIA
MACHINE PIECED, MACHINE APPLIQUED AND MACHINE QUILTED; COTTON, COMBED WOOL

Near her home in Williamstown, Evelyn often watches the 2.4 class yachts sailing. Many of the skippers are friends and are hoping to represent Australia in the Sydney 2000 Paralympic Games. Evelyn used images of these yachts, sailing at the Royal Yacht Club of Victoria, to create *Reaching Towards Sydney 2000*.

Starting with a small photograph, Evelyn enlarged the sails several times, knowing that she just wanted sails, not hulls, in her quilt. She fashioned her extensive collection of blue fabrics into a crazy patchwork background and machine quilted it. She then machine appliqued the sails onto the background. As the final touch, Evelyn couched wool 'waves' around the sails, and spelled out 'Sydney 2000' in signal flags.

Evelyn is an amateur patchworker and quilter, producing thirty quilts since doing a beginner's course in 1992. She exhibits annually with Victoria's Australian Quilters Association, and enjoys investigating new techniques and ideas, although her preference is towards traditional styles of patchwork.

120

172

575

100

4

213

521

36 GATHERING OF FRIENDS
80 CM x 142 CM (32 IN x 57 IN)
BY THE GALAHS, LANE COVE, NEW SOUTH WALES
MACHINE APPLIQUED AND MACHINE QUILTED; COTTON, HAND DYED BACKGROUND FABRIC

John Butler is a Sydney-based naïve painter whose work has a whimsical take on life expressed through birds and animals. The Galahs have along admired his art and, with permission, based their quilt, *Gathering of Friends*, on one of his paintings. The quilt captures the high humour of a group of galahs and kookaburras as they arrive together to raucously discuss the day's activities in an old banksia tree. Long-time students of Dianne Finnegan, the Galahs felt that this image best captured the fun and games at their own weekly meetings.

The eight members of the group made the elements for the quilt, each selecting birds, leaves and tree to fashion ready for applique onto the prepared background fabric. Ruching for the tree trunk gave texture and a sculptural character to the work. Dianne machine quilted the quilt.

The Galahs meet weekly at the home of their teacher, Dianne Finnegan, to share and learn. Often, Dianne sets goals for the group which extend their knowledge and provide them with challenges which they might not attempt as individuals. This is one of three quilts that the Galahs have made for the QUILTS 2000 project. In addition, several members have made individual quilts.

415

† 65

436

463

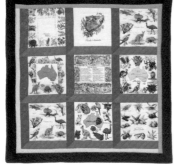

216

74

220

594

69

141

9

383

† 111 UP THE CREEK
101 CM X 119 CM (40 IN X 48 IN)
BY JUDITH CUNEO BURGESS, MONA VALE, NEW SOUTH WALES
MACHINE PIECED, MACHINE APPLIQUED, MACHINE EMBROIDERED AND MACHINE QUILTED; COTTON, VELVET, SYNTHETICS, UPHOLSTERY FABRICS, INKED AND PAINTED DETAILS

Up the Creek takes a whimsical look at Australia's love of sport and competition. Before an Australian bush crowd, the koala, platypus and goanna 'go for gold' in the backstroke finals. Designing as she sewed, Judith was inspired by her grandson, Rowan, who is a champion swimmer. His favourite stroke is backstroke.

For Judith, colour is the most important factor when designing quilts and she will use almost any fabric or technique to achieve just the right effect in her 'pictures'. Here, she combines applique, painting and many different textured fabrics with inventive machine techniques to create a storybook picture of fun in the bush. *Up The Creek* is machine made using raw-edged applique, embellished with machine embroidery. Judith added lines for the claws and fur of the mother koala, and created lifelike eyes for the animals with a combination of embroidery and inked embellishments.

Judith gave up painting, her chosen profession, when introduced to modern quiltmaking in 1980. She loves to combine drawing and painting techniques, making story quilts especially for children. She is an active member of Hunters Hill Quilters and has won 'Best of Show' three times at their annual quilt show.

274

480

168

515

293

† 494

545

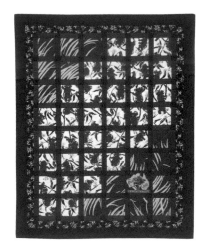

553

354 POSTCARDS FROM THE MIA
118 CM X 118 CM (47 IN X 47 IN)
BY THE MURRUMBIDGEE COUNTRY QUILTERS
HAND PIECED AND HAND APPLIQUED, THREE DIMENSIONAL RUCHING AND EMBROIDERY; COTTON

Inspired by the agricultural, natural and human aspects of the Murrumbidgee Irrigation Area (MIA), members of the Murrumbidgee Country Quilters selected specific industries to feature in sixteen blocks, using their own experiences as a guide. Included are chickens, rice, grape and vegetable growing.

While the rest of the group worked on their blocks, four members worked on the centre medallion which included many forms of applique, three dimensional ruching and hand and machine embroidery.

The Murrumbidgee Country Quilters were formed four years ago. Each year they donate the proceeds from their annual exhibition to charity.

404

104

279

201

† 361

128

520

268

† 367

332

243

337

501 THE BIG DRY #3—EL NINO'S LEGACY
144 CM X 90 CM (57 IN X 36 IN)
BY VAL NADIN, PENNANT HILLS, NEW SOUTH WALES
HAND APPLIQUED AND MACHINE QUILTED; HAND DYED COTTON

This is one of a series of quilts in which Val endeavours to capture the feeling of the Australian outback after a prolonged period of drought, particularly during El Nino. The land is stripped of vegetation and the underlying earth dries and cracks, forming vast expanses of desolation. The islands formed between the cracks are featured in *The Big Dry #3—El Nino's Legacy* in the colours of the Australian landscape, varying from the deep, rich, earthy colours to shades of purple and grey-blue where the shadows fall.

Using hand dyed fabrics, Val has captured the rugged look of the outback setting by using raw-edged, hand applique techniques. Quilting is by machine and echoes the contours of the 'land'.

As well as being an expert traditional quiltmaker, Val designs her own quilts, challenged by the opportunities to incorporate unusual and exotic materials and discover new ways of assembling fabrics. Her work has been exhibited in galleries and exhibitions in Australia, the United States, Japan, and Europe, and has featured in local and overseas publications.

532

327

346

48

45

167

442

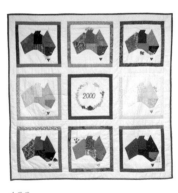

466

564

230

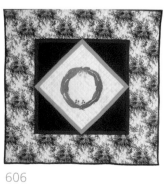

606

592

† 8 **BANKSIAS**
114 CM X 124 CM (46 IN X 49 IN)
BY PAM WINSEN, YERONGA, QUEENSLAND
MACHINE APPLIQUED, MACHINE QUILTED AND MACHINE EMBROIDERED; COTTON, SOME HAND DYED

The banksias cling to the rocky cliffs at Stradbroke Island where the oranges and yellows of this unique flower are offset by the grey-green of the foliage and the clear blue of the Pacific Ocean stretching to the horizon. *Banksias* reflects these images, making a truly dramatic impact. The endurance and success of the banksias growing in inhospitable ground is like the Paralympian athletes' determination and strength of will to succeed.

Pam used free machine embroidery on net over hand dyed fabrics to create the image of the banksias, against a background of blue and aqua fabrics representing the sea and sky.

Pam is a renowned Australian textile artist whose work has been exhibited extensively, including The New Quilt '99—More or Less at the Manly Art Gallery; Making Their Mark in Sydney and Melbourne; Australia Dreaming—Quilts to Nagoya, which toured to Japan; and Colours of Australia, which is currently touring Australia.

158

416

228

565

424

527

96

335

421

197 REDIRECTED
88 CM X 127 CM (35 IN X 51 IN)
BY BARBARA MCCABE, WANGARATTA, VICTORIA
MACHINE APPLIQUE AND MACHINE EMBROIDERY; SHEERS, SYNTHETICS, LAME, POSTAGE STAMPS, PLASTIC

Postage stamps are small reflections of social history. They capture our attention for a brief moment, then are lost after serving the purpose for which they were intended. The images are forgotten—real life pictures and the work of the artists soon gone from memory. Barbara wanted to preserve the many used postage stamps she had, so rather than be forgotten, they could be seen and appreciated once more.

In *Redirected*, Barbara applied strips of colourful and metallic fabrics into place on three separate panels. She sewed small rectangles of plastic over each stamp and covered each panel with organza. Having decorated the entire surface with free machine embroidery and decorative machine stitches, selected areas of organza were carefully cut away—particularly from over the stamps. Each decorative panel can hang alone or be attached to its red background.

Pushing the boundaries of traditional quiltmaking, Barbara's work often includes paper, plastic and beads, as well as a wide variety of fabrics and threads. In 1998, her work was featured on the poster promoting the exhibition, One Step Further, at the National Gallery of Victoria. Her work has featured in many exhibitions including The Running Stitch Contemporary Wool Exhibition and Marvelous Miniatures by the Victorian Quilters' Inc. between 1996 and 1999, winning first prize in 1998. *Redirected* was displayed at The Exhibitions Gallery, Wangaratta during the Stitched Up Textile Festival in 1999, which Barbara instigated and organised.

459

253

151

236

248

214

475

202

329

145

252

PARALYMPICS SYDNEY 2000

402

† **250 RED HEART**
125 cm x 131 cm (50 in x 52 in)
By Lee Cleland, Yamba, New South Wales
Machine pieced and machine quilted; cotton

Reminiscent of old Amish quilts, *Red Heart* captures the essence of these quilts with their simplicity of piecing and juxtaposition of colours, but at the same time, brings an awareness that this is not a traditional quilt. It is a quilt from a new country, for a new country, about a new country. The red heart is for the centre of Australia, the green for the forests and scrub, the mauve for the eucalyptus haze in summer and the blue for the oceans that surround the land.

Having created the combination of simple shapes, Lee redesigned traditional quilting patterns to add texture to the quilt.

Lee Cleland started quilting in 1968 and is now regarded as one of Australia's leading teachers of machine quilting. Her book, *Quilting Makes the Quilt*, has been enormously successful and she is a regular contributor of feature articles to national quilting magazines. Lee has received many major awards for her work, including 'Best of Show' in the Sydney Quilt Festival in 1990. Her quilt was the first machine made quilt to win this coveted award.

493

456

300

435

326

226

542

467

255

544

392

451

† 107 SYDNEY HARBOUR—THE SPIRIT OF SYDNEY
116 CM X 90 CM (46 IN X 36 IN)
BY SUE WADEMAN, QUEENSTOWN, NEW ZEALAND
MACHINE QUILTED AND MACHINE EMBROIDERED; LAYERED RAW-EDGED SILK

Inspired by urban and natural landscapes, and using colour and simple forms as her strongest design elements, Sue creates artwork that evokes an initial reaction and an emotional response. In *Sydney Harbour—The Spirit of Sydney*, she has used a spontaneous collage style to convey the excitement of Sydney and its fabulous harbour in the lead up to the 2000 Games.

In this technique, crudely cut, raw-edged pieces of silk are overlayed and stitched in place, creating a landscape with both form and texture. Selection of fabric was crucial to the success of the final work.

Sue is an internationally acclaimed artist, whose work has been exhibited in the Baroque to Avant Garde Quilt Festival in Innsbruck, Austria; the Textile Museum in Munich, Germany; and Taj Enterprise, Japan. A sought after tutor, Sue has taught fabric collage to students in Japan, America, New Zealand and throughout Australia.

98

† 283

99

153

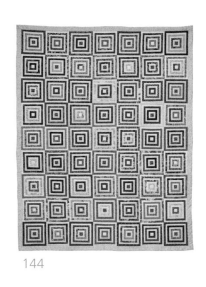

144

525

217

591

604

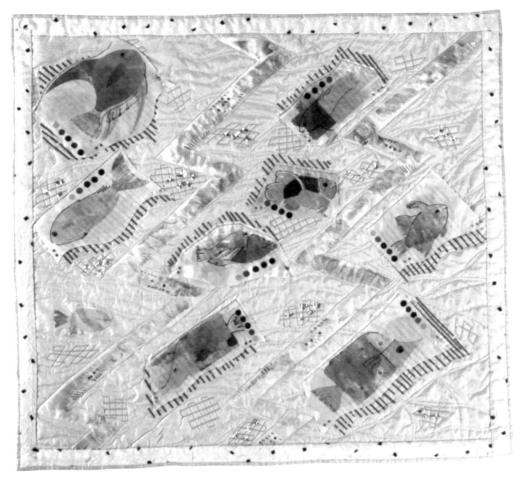

† 6 **PATTERN PENDING**
120 CM X 109 CM (48 IN X 44 IN)
BY MARJORIE COLEMAN, MOFFAT BEACH, QUEENSLAND
TRANSFER DYES AND DRAWINGS, FUSED APPLIQUE; SILK

While snorkelling on tropical reefs, Marjorie was struck by the patterning of the fish. The striking combinations of dots, stripes, chevrons and blocks expressed in such bright and unlikely colour combinations would do the most adventurous fabric designer proud.

To capture this, Marjorie used heat-transfer dyes to create the fish shapes and the light shafts on the water in *Pattern Pending*. Outline drawings were done with permanent felt pens and the coloured dots and the pink decorative stripes were attached with fusible webbing. The free-floating fabric fish were attached with tailors tacks and pins to further a 'value added' notion of fish as fabric design.

A quiltmaker for twenty-six years, Marjorie is concerned with creating rather than copying, and expressing her own surroundings rather than something seen somewhere else. She has had her work published in many reputable quiltmaking books and journals and was the first Australian quiltmaker to be featured in Quilt Digest in 1987. Her work has been included in many exhibitions in Australia and in the United States, Japan, France, Britain and Germany, often by invitation. Private collectors in Australia, France, Japan and the United States have purchased her quilts, as have the National Gallery of Australia in Canberra and the Powerhouse Museum in Sydney.

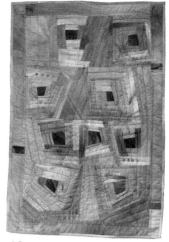

18

195

610

303

343

211

437

149

312

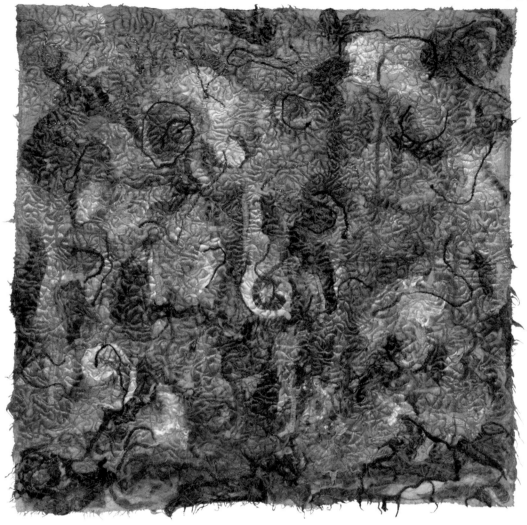

59 A PIROUETTE OF PERFECTLY POISED PARROTS, PURPOSEFULLY PERFORMING & PERSERVERING IN POWERFUL PARTENERSHIP
92 CM X 92 CM (36 IN X 36 IN)
BY GILLIAN HAND, DARGAN, NEW SOUTH WALES
MACHINE AND HAND LAYERED; WOOL, SILK, VARIOUS THREADS

Outside Gillian's bush studio, parrots pirouette and swoop, part of the ever-changing scene of bush colours and textures, providing a constant source of delight and inspiration.

Using faux felt, a technique she has recently developed, Gillian has captured the movement of parrots in the Australian bush by multi-layering and stitching various fabrics, fibres and threads together. Gillian chose faux felt as the medium because it is so luxurious and multi-faceted. There is always something new to catch the eye at each viewing of this quilt. The lustre of silk combines beautifully with the softness of wool in *A Pirouette of Perfectly Poised Parrots* enhanced by the intricacy of threadwork and the harmonious colours.

Gillian Hand has expressed herself through colour, cloth and stitching since she was a young girl. This exploration has taken many forms—currently, she is interested in studying the relevance of sacred art within the context of contemporary society. She plans to explore the search for meaning through the making and using of sacred cloth and mandalas. Gillian has exhibited widely in New South Wales and Victoria, and has recently completed a series of textile art works for Nepean Hospital NSW, working with women from three cultural groups.

432

301

249

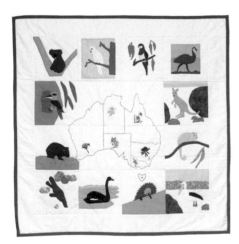

207

196

147

468

574

596

† 87 PARALYMPIANS ARE ALL STARS
95 CM X 102 CM (38 IN X 41 IN)
BY NARELLE GRIEVE, ST IVES, NEW SOUTH WALES
WHOLECLOTH, HAND QUILTED, TRAPUNTO; SYNTHETIC

Being a 'no-exercise' person, Narelle has great admiration for any athlete. However, she feels the Paralympians, who have overcome additional hurdles to become elite athletes, are deserving of special admiration. In *Paralympians Are All Stars*, she captures this feeling.

Known internationally for her wholecloth quilts, it was natural for Narelle to use this medium for *Paralympians Are All Stars*. Beginning with a piece of white synthetic fabric, known throughout Australia as 'Narelle's fabric', she first marked her design in pencil. Using coloured thread for the quilting, Narelle has added subtle shades of colour to the quilt. For the words and the stars, she used trapunto techniques.

Introduced to quiltmaking in 1982, Narelle quickly realised her love of wholecloth quilts and hand quilting. Her work displays a level of perfection achieved by few quilters, making her one of the best hand quilters in the country. Her wholecloth quilts have won her several major awards, including Best of Show in two quilt shows in the United States, at the Royal Easter Show in Sydney in 1987 and 1994, and at the Hunters Hill Quilt Show in 1987.

Narelle is widely sought after as a tutor, judge and lecturer. She is the quilting consultant for a national patchwork magazine, for whom she writes a regular column. Her book, *Collecting Quilts*, was published in 1997, and she regularly takes tours of quiltmakers to the United States.

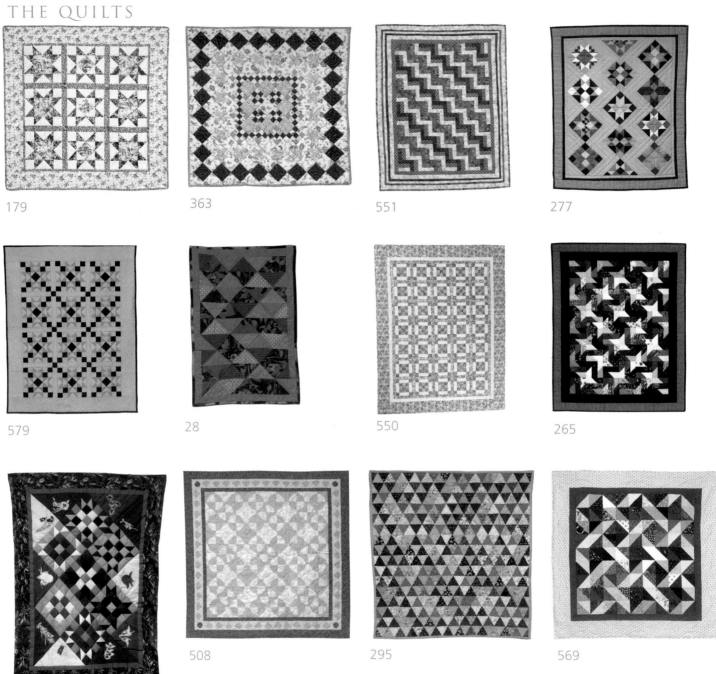

179

363

551

277

579

28

550

265

41

508

295

569

401 DESERT LIGHTS (LEFT)
149 CM X 149 CM (60 IN X 60 IN)
BY MARGARET AITKEN, MOSMAN, NEW SOUTH WALES
MACHINE PIECED AND HAND QUILTED; COTTON

Inspired by the freedom of design and colour in the Cook Islander's Tivaevae and her love of traditional quiltmaking, Margaret chose the traditional Double-T block, using only two colours, to make *Desert Nights*. She enjoys working with time-honoured techniques and delights in the simplicity of an all-over design. Margaret has been quilting for seventeen years, has won several major awards in Australia and is highly sought after for commissioned work.

62 FRILLED (RIGHT)
104 CMX 150 CM (42 IN X 60 IN)
BY MARGIE MAY, STONYFELL, SOUTH AUSTRALIA
MACHINE PIECED AND HAND QUILTED; ALL COTTON

Wanting to wish Australia's elite athletes with a disability every success, Margie made *Frilled*, using the traditional Bright Hopes block. It was her second quilt using this simple block, the first in the series being made for the South Australian Quilters Guild's Exhibition, Towards the New Millenium.

Margie prefers to work with tradtional patterns, allowing her fabric choice to provide a contemporary edge to her work. In *Frilled*, she added a border of triangles to the pieced top, reminiscent of the frill on Lizzie, the frill-necked lizard, mascot for the Sydney 2000 Paralympic Games.

THE QUILTS

231

388

431

414

510

488

365

94

142

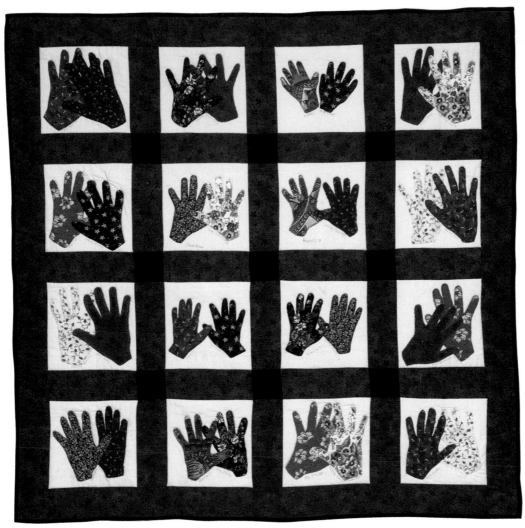

† 108 OUR HELPING HANDS
137 CM X 137 CM (55 IN X 55 IN)
BY I.O. CLASS, TEMORA WEST PUBLIC SCHOOL, TEMORA, NEW SOUTH WALES
HAND APPLIQUED, TIED; COTTON

Inspired by stories of athletes training for the Sydney 2000 Paralympic Games, the children at Temora West intellectually challenged class, set about making a quilt to donate to QUILTS 2000. Although they had never made a quilt before, they were very enthusiastic and soon were choosing fabrics and learning new skills from their teacher, Rosemary Small.

On each child's 'hand' block is embroidered the maker's name and the name of the athlete to whom the block is dedicated. The children chose their athlete because they were involved in a sport in which the maker was interested, or because they shared the same disability. They chose the school colours of maroon and black for the strips joining the blocks and these colours also provided the colour theme for the quilt. The children made a second quilt which they donated to their school.

Many of the children in the class suffer from autism, a condition which prevents their normal response to social interaction and sensory stimuli. Often, they are unable to participate in group activities. One girl had been completely unresponsive, but was able to participate in making a block. Another boy became a 'helper' — a role he had never taken before—assisting a latecomer to the project.

583

469

412

155

517

340

173

146

267

246

† 400

462

127 GOOD NEIGHBOURHOOD
107 CM X 99 CM (43 IN X 39 IN)
BY PATRICIA ROLFE, KOOTINGAL, NEW SOUTH WALES
BLANKET-STITCHED APPLIQUE, HAND QUILTED; COTTON

Patricia's son, David, is an aspiring paralympian who hopes to compete in the Sydney 2000 Paralympic Games. After loosing a leg in an accident seven years ago, David resumed his interest in competitive swimming, something he hadn't done since he was a child. He holds the Australian record for 150 m (165 yd) freestyle. Fourth in the world in this event, he is hoping for a medal at the games. This will be his last chance to compete in the Paralympic Games, as he is thirty-six years old.

After her retirement from nursing, Patricia learned to make quilts and particularly enjoys applique, using a technique her daughter showed her. In *Good Neighbourhood*, she designed an Australian country community with people, farms and native animals all living happily together. As her quilt developed, her own neighbourhood got involved, giving advice on what should be added next.

When her last child left home for university, Patricia decided to broaden her own horizons, beginning with Glenys Mann's patchwork classes in Tamworth. She is particularly fond of decorating her home with country quilts and other cottage crafts, such as candlewicking. Patricia's work has won several awards through the local Country Women's Association, of which she was a co-founder.

452

538

504

134

470

552

121

379

123

352

549

534

238 MAGPIES AND WATTLE
140 CM X 142 CM (56 IN X 57 IN)
BY THE QUEANBEYAN QUILTERS INC, QUEANBEYAN, NEW SOUTH WALES
MACHINE PIECED, HAND APPLIQUED, HAND QUILTED; COTTON

The Queanbeyan Quilters are a generous group of quilters. Each year they make a quilt to be used by a local charity to raise funds. In 1999, they decided to donate their quilt to QUILTS 2000 to raise funds for the Sydney 2000 Paralympic Games.

After much discussion, patterns from a Hetty van Boven book, *From Australia with Love,* were selected for the magpie and wattle blocks. Templates and fabric packs were prepared, ready for the workshop day, when fifteen members worked together to machine piece the blocks. The quilt top was marked with long eucalyptus leaves and sandwiched ready for quilting, which was undertaken by five other members of this very active group.

In their local town, Queanbeyan Quilters are well-known for their delightful Bicentennial Quilt, created in 1988, which is on public display. The group made another bicentennial quilt for Hatta, Queanbeyan's sister city in Japan.

386

477

316

444

399

602

375

14

531

390

148

182

140 DAWN IN THE HIGH COUNTRY
70 cm x 90 cm (28 in x 36 in)
By Susan Cooper, Wangi Wangi, New South Wales
Machine pieced colourwash; cotton

Kosciusko National Park, with its delightful countryside, mountain flora, tussock grasses, snow-melt streams and majestic ranges is the subject of *Dawn in the High Country*. During Spring, Susan enjoyed a trail ride though this magnificent Australian park and observed many of the flowering plants along the path were flowering, thriving despite the harsh terrain. She felt that their survival in such extremes of climate parallel the success of the Paralympians who have to overcome extreme difficulties to achieve their goals.

Susan finds using colourwash techniques to create beautiful landscapes a liberating experience that is limited only by imagination and her fabric stash. Originally taught by her mother, quiltmaker Marcia Hoipo, she now specialises in making colourwash quilts. With a theme in mind, she starts the design process by collecting fabrics and deciding on the dimensions of the quilt. Using an extensive design wall covered with cotton wadding, she 'plays' with the squares of fabric to create a landscape. For *Dawn in the High Country*, the stream was central to the design and was completed first.

Susan is a highly sought after tutor, conducting many weekend workshops in her local community and has had several articles about her work published in a national patchwork magazine. As a member of the Facets textile gallery in Pokolbin, NSW, Susan's work is exhibited with several other textile artists.

540

310

280

232

457

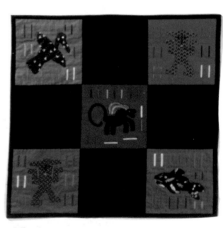

35

509

86

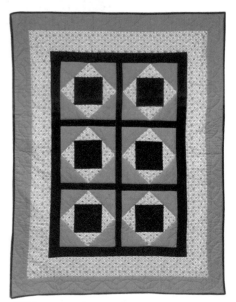

396

7 THE CALM BEFORE ...
117 CM X 120 CM (47 IN X 48 IN)
BY CHOY-LIN WILLIAMS, KURRAJONG HEIGHTS, NEW SOUTH WALES
HAND APPLIQUED AND HAND QUILTED; SILK, COTTON AND SYNTHETICS

Just before a storm, nature seems to calm, sensing the imminent rush of energy about to engulf it. *The Calm Before ...* captures this mood. Choy-Lin likens it to that moment just before competition when athletes have to focus their thoughts, energy and attention on their goal—to win!

Choy-Lin has made several quilts using this method, where she hand appliques strips into place, rather than strip piecing them. She then hand quilts, using sashiko thread to add surface texture.

A quilter since 1987, Choy-Lin has been exhibiting her quilts nationally and internationally since 1989. She has won many prizes, including the Noreen Dunn Memorial Award for Excellence in Quilting at the Quilters' Guild Exhibition in 1990, and second prize in the Fruits of the Hawkesbury Textile and Fibre Art Exhibition in 1996, 1997 and 1998.

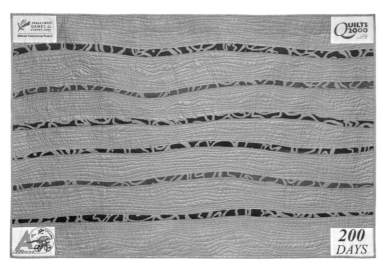

614—200 Days To Go

613—300 Days To Go

620—9 Days To Go

617—50 Days To Go

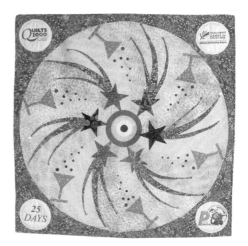

618—25 Days To Go

612—400 Days To Go

616—75 Days To Go

611—500 Days To Go

Unavailable at publication time:
10 DAYS TO GO, by Carolyn Sullivan; 8 DAYS TO GO, by Choy-Lin Williams; 7 DAYS TO GO, by Alysoun Ryves; 6 DAYS TO GO, by Margaret Rolfe; 5 DAYS TO GO, by Jane Gibson; 4 DAYS TO GO, by Avalon Quilters; 3 DAYS TO GO by Mavis Schicht; and 1 DAY TO GO, by Dianne Finnegan

627—2 Days To Go

615—100 Days to Go

INDEX BY QUILT NUMBER

INDEX BY QUILT NUMBER

INDEX BY QUILT NUMBER

INDEX BY QUILT NUMBER

INDEX BY QUILT NUMBER

INDEX BY QUILTMAKER

INDEX BY QUILTMAKER

INDEX BY QUILTMAKER

NOTES

NOTES

FOR THE
SYDNEY 2000
PARALYMPIC GAMES

Many thanks to the following people for their contribution to the book

Managing Editor: Karen Fail

Authors: Dianne Finnegan and Karen Fail

Production Manager, Artwork and Layout: Jan T Urquhart (Utopia Publishing)

Consulting Editors: Judy Poulos, Frances Kenneley Stephenson

Design: Liz Seymour (Seymour Designs)

Data Management: Choy-Lin Williams

Data entry: Jane Gibson, Julie Woods

Proof readers: Cecelia and William Clarke (CFC Research Services)

Photography: Andrew Payne, Oliver Ford, (Photograhix) for the quilts, Terry Finnegan for installation shots.